Gooseberry Patch Co.

A Country Store In Your Mailbox®

Patchwork Potluck

A Country Store In Your Mailbox®

Gooseberry Patch
600 London Road
P.O. Box 190
Delaware, OH 43015

♥

1·800·854·6673
www.gooseberrypatch.com

Do you have a tried & true recipe...

tip, craft or memory that you'd like to see featured in a **Gooseberry Patch** book? Visit our website at **www.gooseberrypatch.com**, register and follow the easy steps to submit your favorite family recipe.
Or send them to us at:

Gooseberry Patch
Attn: Book Dept.
P.O. Box 190
Delaware, OH 43015

Don't forget to include the number of servings your recipe makes, plus your name, street address, phone number and e-mail address. If we select your recipe, your name will appear right along with it...and you'll receive a **FREE** copy of the book!

Contents

Dedication

Dedicated to moms, dads, grandmas, grandpas, aunts, uncles, cousins and of course, their kids...a patchwork quilt of love.

Appreciation

Thanks to everyone who opened up their hearts and their recipe boxes!

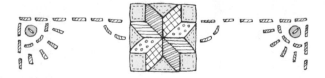

Tina Knotts
Gooseberry Patch

I have many fond memories of the summers my brother and I spent at our Grandma & Grandpa Cushman's house. Our summers were filled with gardening, canning and freezing, and the biggest highlight by far was the county fair. As far back as I can remember, my grandmother would take all of her prized possessions to the fair. She'd enter a giant vegetable basket filled to the brim with fresh tomatoes, potatoes, cabbage, green beans, peppers, carrots, cucumbers and anything else that was ripe. Grandma carefully packed quart jars of green beans, pickled beets and homemade jams & jellies, just about everything she had canned the previous fall. You would think I would remember the rides, sticky cotton candy and the blue snowcones…but what I remember the most is the sparkle in Grandma's eyes when she carried home her county fair entries embellished with blue ribbons.

Teresa Stiegelmeyer
Indianapolis, IN

It makes me so happy to recall a summer farm breakfast with my Grandpa. We went out early in the morning and picked a nice, ripe cantaloupe, fresh and warm from the field. We cut it into halves and scooped out the seeds, filled each cavity with vanilla ice cream and ate it on the back porch before Grandma got up!

Good-Time Memories

Wanda Wilson
Hamilton, GA

Our most memorable picnic was on the 4th of July in 1976, America's bicentennial year. My husband and I, along with our 3 young sons, attended a celebration in Westville, a restored 1800's town. Jimmy Carter, soon to be president, was the speaker. As soon as his rousing speech ended, rain began to fall and we dashed for our station wagon. My husband drove for miles, hoping (but failing) to find a dry spot for our picnic. When hunger pangs overrode common sense, he pulled over into an open field. I crawled into the back of the station wagon and dispensed the traditional fried chicken, corn on the cob and potato salad to everyone. We finished up with chocolate cake, of course. After heading home, I decided to make the day really unforgettable by serving watermelon! You've never lived (or been truly foolish) until you've eaten watermelon at 55 miles per hour! The watermelon seed spitting contest was the best part of the day, even though I vacuumed seeds for months...it's one picnic we have never forgotten!

Julia Gorrell
Xenia, IL

My mother, 2 of my brothers and I were preparing food for our 4th of July picnic in 1976. Mother and the boys were working on the potato salad. I was only 5 at the time and was on a chair at the stove, constantly stirring the coconut frosting for the German chocolate cake. Mother was good delegating in the kitchen...she had to be, with a family of 7! Mother was explaining something to the boys as she chopped the celery for the potato salad. When she finished, she promptly came over to where I was stirring, and scraped the celery into the frosting! I kept trying to interrupt, "Mom..." "I'm talking, sweetie," she'd say. "But Mom..." By the time she was done explaining, the boys realized what she had done and were laughing. She looked at me and I finally got to say, "But Mom, the celery goes in the potato salad." Mom and the boys worked to rescue the celery as best they could. The next day, when we brought out the cake for our picnic, the rest of the family had no clue! I did spot one piece of celery on the cake...I picked it off when no one was looking.

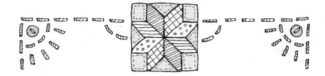

Dianna Likens
Gooseberry Patch

My grandma used to take my twin brother and me strawberry-picking every spring, as soon as he and I were old enough to carry a bucket. The bushes were taller than we were! I'll always remember squinting up at my grandma in the morning sunshine, the dew on the toes of my shoes, and my brother sneaking berries out of my bucket. Although we probably ate almost as many as we picked, we filled those blue rubber buckets as full as we could carry. Back at home, Grandma made jars and jars of strawberry preserves, shortcakes piled high with whipped cream, and froze the rest for rainy days.

Holly Muster
Mount Gilead, OH

"School's out, school's out, teacher let the monkeys out!" When you're a kid, summer is the best time of year. I think it even beats Christmas and your birthday. Why? Because you've just finished 9 months of work and freedom is at your doorstep. Staying up late...for 3 whole months! The street I lived on as a child was a brick dead-end street, but it was far from being dead. The street was filled with the neighborhood kids riding their bikes with banana seats and playing cards clipped near the tires to sound like motors. We would stay up late and get up early. We couldn't let any of our new free time go to waste. I would wake up before the sun made the earth bake like a French fry forgotten in the bottom of the oven. I would sit on the front porch swing in my pajamas and enjoy the cool morning air. I'd watch maybe an hour of cartoons on TV and then head outside for the rest of the day. That was the life!

Good-Time Memories

Karen Adams
Cincinnati, OH

Our family reunions were always on my mother's side of the family. We city folk had to travel the long 4-hour drive to join our country relatives at this once-a-year event. The reunion was always in July, after church on a Sunday. It seems that the weather was always great on that special day! We would have so much food that at least 5 wooden picnic tables would be filled, bursting at the seams with homemade chicken & dumplings, corn canned from the wives' gardens and every fattening dessert ever thought of. We kids would be off exploring and wondering how soon we could get our hands on all that great food. The men would play horseshoes and "shoot the breeze." The women of the family would be catching up on all the family gossip since the last reunion. At last we could eat! The food was so good, it seemed as though none of us had eaten for days. Afterwards we were so full…but we were all happy and glad to be with our family. Although I haven't been to a reunion in years, I think how fortunate I was, to experience such a special event with such a marvelous, caring family full of love and food!

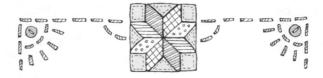

Lily Rivera
Vista, CA

I have many special memories of growing up as one of 10 children in a farming family. Our house was a ramshackle one-bedroom with mattresses spread end to end on one side of the room. Although we were poor, I didn't feel we were lacking anything. My mother's constant quote was, "As long as we have a roof over our heads and food to eat, we are rich!" I can still remember the feeling of "pain" at hearing the rooster crowing in the morning, because I knew soon my father's footsteps would come to rouse us to work in the fields. Sleepily, each of us would climb into the back of our little pickup truck, stumbling over each other to find space for a nap before we reached the field, only to be jostled awake by the pits and ditches in the dirt road that signaled our arrival. Although the rows of sugar peas waiting to be picked were fairly serious business, we made up games while we worked, much to my father's disapproval, racing each other to the end of the rows, singing songs, and playing with the little insects which visited occasionally…dragonflies being my favorite. Looking back, our lives were filled with beauty, nature and adventure which replaced the need for material possessions.

⊙✗✗ Good-Time Memories ✗✗⊙

Tammy Kling
Howard, PA

I remember homemade ice cream at Gram's house, where all the family would gather on a Saturday night for supper. After supper we would all help with dishes and then we would make homemade ice cream. Some of us would go down and chip ice off the side of the mountain when the water had run down and frozen in the cold winter air. We would take the ice back to Gram's and then we all took turns cranking the ice cream maker in the big wooden tub. It got really hard to turn before the ice cream was almost done. And then we got to eat

it…oh, it was so soft and yummy. It melted so fast in your mouth. If you ate it too fast, Gram would tell us, "You'll get a headache." We learned this the hard way! I sure miss the days back then. We still have recipes from Gram to this day that our family uses each holiday.

Melody Somers
West Milford, WV

From the time I was 3 years old through 5th or 6th grade, I had a babysitter whose name was Orpha. She was about 60 years old then (40 years ago) and lived in a very old house. She had the coldest, cleanest well water, which she used for everything. She would draw the water and heat it up for my sponge baths whenever I would stay the night with her. She had old pictures of family members hanging above the beds in frames covered with heavy beveled glass. She would play the antique Victrola. Every time I would go to Orpha's house, it smelled like fresh-baked cookies. She baked raisin oatmeal cookies almost every day and there were always fresh ones in the cookie jar…literally an old Mason jar that sat at the bottom of a shelf. To this day, I can smell those cookies and remember the peace I felt when I would stay with Orpha.

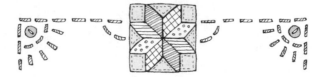

Stella Hickman
Gooseberry Patch

My grandma, Marjorie Love, was 80 in 1966 when she made her last Love baby quilt for her grandson, Shawn. The family tradition was to make a crib-size quilt in the Cradle pattern, with alternating pink and blue pieces. Grandma edged it in blue, as most Love babies were boys. Grandma herself had 11 boy babies and only one daughter. Grandma Love was a country woman from Caldwell, Ohio and had lived on a hillside farm her whole life. She was devout and loving, kissing each cradle piece and saying a prayer for the baby as she stitched. Her hands were gnarled and rough from working her one-acre garden every day, and it took her the better part of a year to complete Shawn's quilt. Grandma took delight in holding baby Shawn in his quilt and rocking him in her parlor. Today Shawn and his wife, Holly, have 2 sons, Tyler and Taner. Both in turn have been wrapped and rocked in that warm little quilt made by their great-grandmother. That sweet quilt will be passed on to more Love children.

Pat Bowers
Rome, NY

When I was growing up, my family would go to my grandparents' house on Sundays for dinner. Gramps would cook "chicken & dumplin's." Oh, was it gooood! While Gramps was cooking the dumplings, he said we couldn't make any noise or the dumplings wouldn't rise. We would all tiptoe and whisper and never ever let the door slam. Even the lid had to be placed gently on the pot, or disaster would strike. When I was almost 20 and wanted to learn to make chicken & dumplin's, I learned from my mother that the necessity for quiet had absolutely nothing to do with the dumplings not rising...rather, it was a really effective way of having a little peace & quiet in the house before dinner. Gramps, you still make me smile when I serve your chicken & dumplin's!

Good-Time Memories

Kristie Rigo
Friedens, PA

My grandmother grew up during the Depression and nothing was ever wasted. She could take leftovers and make a meal fit for a king. She could roast a chicken for Sunday dinner, and the following week we'd have chicken salad sandwiches, chicken pot pie and chicken & gravy over waffles, and no one ever complained about leftovers! In my favorite memories of Grandma Beal, I almost always think of sitting in her huge dining room playing games and laughing and eating. Her dining room was so large that she had 2 tables in it...one for dinner and one for breakfast, lunch, game playing or sitting around listening to stories. Her kitchen was long and narrow, with a refrigerator filled with goodies and an old stove that always had something simmering on top. Everyone knew that when you visited Grandma, you would be eating something, because she wouldn't take no for an answer! And honestly, I don't think anyone ever wanted to say no. Sometimes when I'm preparing a meal that she used to make, I think back to those days and feel blessed that she was a part of my life.

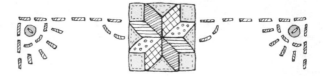

Donna Shafer
Genoa, OH

For the last few years the Cress family has gotten together each July, much to the delight of my Grandpa Joe. Everyone starts arriving at our house on Thursday and we wrap up on Sunday. We have over 30 people, 9 dogs and one cat, and we just pile in and sleep wherever we can. Some bring tents to set up in the yard. Saturday night, after a great day of swimming and boating, is when we have our big shindig, and that's when we really start having fun! Whatever the theme is, we run with it, from the invitations to the contest prizes. One year we had a Luau theme with a treasure hunt, hula hoop & limbo contests, tiki bar and great foods like kabobs on the grill, sweet bread and homemade ice cream. Another year we had a 1950's theme with a soda-shop flair serving hamburgers, hot dogs, fries, floats and my Uncle Carl's cherry pie, just like Grandma Cress used to make. We dress up according to the theme, and everyone really does a great job with their outfits, with the best winning a prize. Family reunions make for great photo opportunities with your family that you don't get to see very often, along with memories that will last a lifetime! My mom and I enjoy scrapbooking all of the photos and everyone gets a kick out of looking at them the following summer.

⊘✗✗ Good-Time Memories ✗✗⊘

Angie McFarland
Brandon, IA

My Grandma Pearl was one of the best bakers I know. If you ask any of her kids, grandkids or great-grandkids for one memory of her that they all shared in common, I know every one of them would mention baking with her, or eating her goodies. She always had time to whip up a coffee cake, cinnamon rolls, cookies or banana bread for someone who needed nourishment or just a bit of love. I learned most of my baking skills at her side, and still use them today. Thankfully, my daughter got to spend time in the kitchen with her, and one of her favorite pictures is of Great-Gramma Pearl and her making sugar cookies together. Today, when I feel the need for a hug from a grandma who is no longer here, I get out the cookbook she gave me, turn to one of her tried & true recipes, get out the baking pans that she always used, and mix up a batch of love.

Debbie Talbott
Columbus, OH

My great-great-grandma baked pies for a bakery for most of her working life. Maw-Maw was well-known in the community for baking the "best-ever" pies. When she baked for the bakery, as well as for her family, she never measured anything. When she got very old and we knew her baking days were numbered, her granddaughter wanted to make sure her pies would live on, so one day she accompanied Maw-Maw in the kitchen for a baking day. As Maw-Maw took a handful of this, a pinch of that, her granddaughter lovingly took Maw-Maw's hand and led it to a bowl, where she measured each ingredient that was to be used in each pie. Now, to this day, her family is able to enjoy a pie that is "nearly as good as Grandma made."

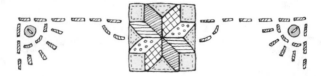

Thais Menges
Three Rivers, MI

There are many "Special Days" in this world if we will just make family & friends a priority. I want to tell you about one of mine. My sister, Peg, called me one morning and told me to get ready, she was picking me up, but wouldn't tell me where we were going or what we were going to do. What fun to know that something different was going to happen on an otherwise ho-hum day! She arrived with a big smile on her face as we started driving to a destination that only she knew. Several miles down the road, we came to an enchanting little park with stately trees and a cascading waterfall that bubbled into a stream. There she opened the trunk of her car and grasped a bountiful picnic basket. As we sat in the warm sun, she laid out scrumptious sandwiches, fresh tomatoes, cookies and thirst-quenching ice tea. What a delight it was to talk and laugh the afternoon away, and to feel like giggling little girls once more. What a marvelous gift she gave me on that warm summer day. I will hold it in my heart forever!

Corky Hines
Walworth, NY

I grew up in the 1950's in an old house with a primitive shower that was difficult for a youngster to use. So on Saturdays my younger sister, Joanne, and I would go to our Grandma Karstedt's house and take a bath in her beautiful porcelain bathtub. After a thorough soak in the tub, we would play with the paper dolls Grandma saved us from her *McCall's* magazines and she would curl our hair in rags so we would look pretty for Sunday School the next day. Grandma would serve us lunch on her ruby glass dishes, which I always thought were very special. I didn't realize they had been given out as premiums at gas stations. Today I collect ruby glass myself to pass down to my daughters someday in memory of my grandma who passed away before they were born.

⊘✕✕ Good-Time Memories ✕✕⊘

Carla Whittier
Lexington, SC

Every summer, my parents, sisters and I would all load up in the family Explorer and head north to Wisconsin and Minnesota for a week of fishing. Some of the best memories I have are of the 5 of us in that fishing cabin and on the lake. I remember sitting in the boat with my father on the lake at 5 or 6 in the morning, watching the sun rise while fishing on a glassy lake. We were discussing religion and spirituality, and I don't think there could have been anything more spiritual than that particular moment…perfectly picturesque and serene. I also remember my sisters and me resetting our father's alarm from 5 to 3 in the morning. He was all dressed and ready to go fishing when he realized it was still dark outside! Luckily for us, he went back to bed and didn't wake us up! I remember doing more laughing and giggling in the boat with my mom than actually fishing. When we think about it now, we really aren't surprised that we didn't catch anything. My family still goes fishing for one week each summer, only now we get 2 cabins instead of one, to accommodate husbands and children. We still have fun, laugh, giggle and play the occasional prank or joke on Daddy.

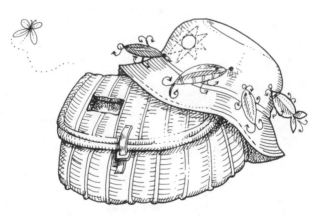

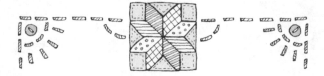

Wendy Carl
Red Lion, PA

My Grandma Weeks would serve us grandkids "coffee soup" for breakfast. Most of us lived close by, so you never knew who else would be at the table. Sometimes there would be as many as 5 or 6 kids all unannounced and hungry for coffee soup, which our mothers never made at home. So simple…place a slice of homemade bread on a plate, pour some hot coffee over it and sprinkle with sugar. Summer held another special Grandma treat, popsicles made of juices left from Grandma's home-canned peaches and pears. Her freezer opened at the bottom (perfect for us kids) and every surface held popsicles. We could have as many as we wanted (just return the spoons and sticks, please!). We trooped through Grandma's house from attic to basement, played dress-up in my aunt's old clothes and shoes, took every salt shaker in the kitchen out into the yard to eat green apples off her trees, and rarely gave her a day's quiet. Grandma passed away in 1990. We all miss her so much, but over 200 of us come to our reunion every summer. We share stories of the things we did at Grandma's house and remember how good it felt to be there.

Shana Still
Jacksonville, FL

For 20 years my Aunt Debbie, Granny and I have taken trips to the Smoky Mountains. We always stopped for lunch at this particular picnic bench next to a mountain stream. My granny would pull out the picnic basket and start to get lunch ready as my aunt and I would go to play in the stream. We always ate Granny's famous tomato sandwiches…mayo on both slices of bread, peeled tomatoes, salt & pepper to taste and always cut lengthwise. We would eat potato chips and a cold glass of cola. It was always so great. We always looked forward to that part of the trip. Now that I am married, I try to carry on the tradition with my husband and son, but for some reason the tomato sandwiches never taste as good as they do when Granny makes them. I guess I'll learn in time…but I still don't think mine will ever taste as great as Granny's!

Belinda Mansfield
Limerick, ME

When I was 8 years old, 40 years ago, I went to a reunion of my grandmother's with her sisters and their families. All together, there had to have been about 75 people there. It was in Kingfield, Maine, on top of Freeman's Ridge at the farm where Gram grew up. I played in the barns and in the fields. The air was sweet. I climbed rock walls wondering if my gram had climbed them when she was a girl. I met cousins and second cousins. There were tables and tables of food, all homemade, from pickles to pies. Later I learned most of the dishes were Depression glass. We ate outside at long tables…everyone was smiling and laughing. Life was good!

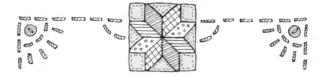

Bobbie Music
Castle Rock, WA

I have the very best memories of my paternal grandmother. We called her Nannie. I LOVED being at her and Papap's house! No matter what we were doing, whether shelling peas, talking on the back porch, picking flowers from her cutting garden, walking to the swimming pool or simply watching TV together, I have never since felt so loved and important as Nannie made me feel. She taught me to fry an egg, make coleslaw and embroider...she even made sure my tin was always stocked with embroidery floss and teatowels or pillowcases. I guess that any time I spent with Nannie was memorable, from the time I was born through adulthood.

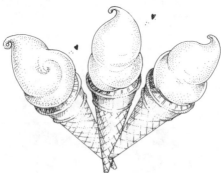

Angie Pontius
Bloomington, IL

My grandpa was a switchman for the Nickel Plate Railroad and has always retained his love of trains, although he is still partial to steam engines! When my brother and I were young, he would call and ask if we were ready to go see the train. Being ready meant that we had eaten dinner, taken baths and changed into our pajamas. We watched out the window waiting for Pa and Nana to pull into the driveway, and would dash to the car when we saw them. On the way to the train station, we would stop at an ice cream shop and would always get an ice cream cone with lemon soft-serve, because the lemon was Pa's favorite. Then we would drive to the train station and eat our ice cream as we watched the train pull into the station. To this day, when I go to that ice cream shop, I get the lemon soft-serve...because it's Pa's favorite.

Good-Time Memories

Cynnamon Kiser
Longmont, CO

We go every year to the Conner family reunion in late July. It is held on the top of Bent Mountain in Check, Virginia, at the house built in 1876 where my husband's grandfather was born. Sometimes we go up a few days before the Sunday reunion and sleep in the house. It has a tin roof so when it rains, it is so peaceful. When everybody arrives on Sunday, the ladies take all the food to the kitchen. When it's dinner time, they ring the bell and we all line up at the front porch, file in, grab a plate and head into the kitchen to get a plate full of that good Southern food, then go out the back of the house. After we eat, some of the men go to the natural spring near the house and retrieve about 5 watermelons that have been getting nice and cold. Once everyone has had their fill, we have a gospel sing on the front porch. All the great-grandparents sit on the porch and sing the old hymns...their children get up and sing with them. It is such a memorable time of food, family and history.

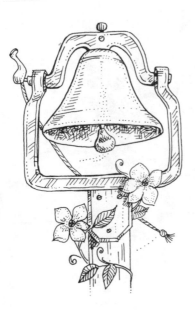

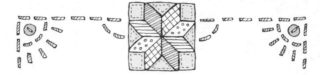

Flo Burtnett
Gage, OK

When the spring days begin to grow warm and the wild plants begin to grow, I remember my childhood and the times when Mother and I would gather wild greens. Early in the morning, Mother would get a tin bucket and a knife. She would put on her flowered sunbonnet made from feedsacks and we would start down the road to gather lamb's quarters and thistles…green and tender, just right for picking. Mother would push her knife under each plant and cut off its roots. When the bucket was full, we would go back to the house and wash the greens. Then she would cook them in water, adding a little salt. A little vinegar poured over the greens, just before eating, made them so delicious. She often served the lamb's quarters and thistles with corn-bread and pinto beans. Dad especially loved these wild greens. I don't pick lamb's quarters myself anymore, but when I see them popping through the ground in the spring it brings back childhood memories.

Good-Time Memories

Phyllis Peters
Three Rivers, MI

My mother-in-law, Ella, was a farm wife who never went without an apron. In the early morning Ella slipped the apron over her head and began daily duties for her family. Getting the fire started, the apron held kindling to spark the blaze. The outer sides of the apron pulled together made a pouch to hold chicken feed. When she gathered eggs she carried them in a convenient basket, the colored apron. If chickens escaped the wire fence, the apron was fanned to rush the fowl back to the henhouse. When the noon meal was ready, Ella summoned Grandpa in from the field with the apron held high. Grandbabies visited and she amused them with a peekaboo game behind the apron. Occasionally it also dried their tears. Happy memories come to mind as I remember a truly wonderful mother by marriage, and her lovely assortment of aprons that were such a part of her life.

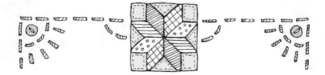

Kris Coburn
Dansville, NY

For my grandmother's 80th birthday, I decided to make her a memory book. I wrote to her family & friends, asking them to write Grandma a letter telling of their favorite memories they had shared with her. I also requested any old pictures they might have. The response was over-whelming! People sent birthday cards and the great-grandchildren drew pictures. I had never scrapbooked before, but went to the craft store and bought supplies, along with a large scrapbook. About a month before Grandma's birthday, we found out that she was terminally ill and might not make it to her birthday. My best friend and I pulled 2 all-nighters to finish the book early. We put all of the letters and pictures into the book just as they were received. It turned out PERFECT! I gave the book to Gram a few weeks early and she was so touched…she spent her last days asking us to read the book to her over and over. I believe that she left us truly knowing what she meant to her family & friends.

⊙ ✕ ✕ Good-Time Memories ✕ ✕ ⊙

Elaine Haworth
Alexandria, LA

I am one of 10 children, 5 boys and 5 girls, ranging in age from 43 to 65 years old. I wanted to do something special for all of them, so a couple years ago, I started jotting down memories of our childhood. I included stories that our 87-year-old mother shared with me, and quotes or sayings that our late father was known for. Each time I thought of something, I would write it down and place it in an envelope for that sibling. Eventually I transferred the memories from the envelopes to large glass jars with a message attached: *"Dear __, I tried to recall memories of our childhood. Some memories are sketchy and humorous, while others may be lengthy and not at all what you recall. There is no order. Read at your pleasure."* My brothers and sisters tell me that they have laughed and cried when reading the memories in their jars. I am now working on memory jars for our daughter, grandson, nieces and nephews. I hope these ideas will inspire others to do something similar for their loved ones.

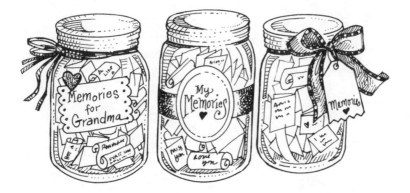

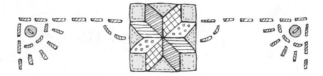

Kathy Hoover
Hobart, IN

My mother-in-law has been in a nursing home with Alzheimer's for several years. Recently we also moved my father-in-law into an assisted-living apartment. While cleaning out their house, we found her wedding gown and veil. They weren't in very good shape, but I just couldn't see them going to a thrift shop. Then it came to me…I would use the fabric and buttons from her gown, as well as the lace and flowers from her veil. For each of my grandchildren, I made a ringbearer's pillow. The grandsons also received cummerbunds, while granddaughters also received garters. On Christmas Eve, when the family was all together, I presented the special gifts. I enclosed a photo of the happy couple on their wedding day in 1944. There wasn't a dry eye in the house! I know my mother-in-law would be so very happy, knowing that her wedding gown will be passed on.

Let's Pack a Picnic Basket

Packable sandwiches & finger foods

Grandma K's Coffee Cake

Sharon Timmerman
Aviston, IL

My grandma always made this coffee cake for a treat when my mom & my aunt came to help her put a new quilt in the frame...it became known as Grandma K's Quilting Coffee Cake.

1/2 c. margarine, softened	2 eggs
1 c. sugar	1 c. sour cream
1 t. vanilla extract	1-1/2 c. all-purpose flour
1/4 t. salt	1 t. baking soda

Blend together margarine, sugar, vanilla and salt in a mixing bowl. Add eggs and mix well. Add sour cream, flour and baking soda. Pour half of batter into a greased 13"x9" baking pan; sprinkle with half of the topping. Pour other half of batter into pan and top with the remaining topping. Bake for 30 minutes at 325 degrees. Makes 16 to 18 servings.

Topping:

1/2 c. sugar	1-1/2 t. cinnamon
1/4 c. chopped nuts	

Mix ingredients well.

Take your family to a nearby park at sunrise for a breakfast picnic filled with rosy skies and singing birds...you'll have the park all to yourselves!

Let's Pack a Picnic Basket

Breakfast Casserole

Jennifer Clingan
Dayton, OH

Prepare this the night before...when you get up in the morning, just pop it in the oven and tote it along in an insulated container.

6 slices bread, torn into bite-size pieces
1 lb. sausage, browned and drained

1 doz. eggs
1/3 c. sour cream
8-oz. pkg. shredded Cheddar cheese

Arrange pieces of bread in the bottom of a greased 13"x9" baking dish. Spread sausage over bread; set aside. Mix eggs and sour cream in a blender until smooth; pour over sausage. Sprinkle cheese over top; cover and bake at 350 degrees for 50 minutes. Remove cover and bake an additional 10 minutes. Serves 6 to 8.

Decoupage favorite photos from family picnics onto a vintage picnic basket. Use paint pens to add family members' names and dates of most-memorable picnics...save room for future memories!

Oatmeal-Blueberry Muffins

Karen Norman
Jacksonville, FL

These muffins are my kids' favorites!

1 egg, beaten
1 c. buttermilk
1/2 c. brown sugar, packed
1/3 c. butter, melted
1 c. quick-cooking oats,
   uncooked

1 c. all-purpose flour
1 t. baking powder
1/2 t. baking soda
1 t. salt
1 c. blueberries

Combine egg, buttermilk, brown sugar and butter; beat well. Mix in oats, flour, baking powder, baking soda and salt just until moistened. Fold in blueberries. Fill 12 greased muffin tins two-thirds full. Bake at 400 degrees for 20 minutes. Makes one dozen.

Ham & Cheese Muffins

Kathy Grashoff
Fort Wayne, IN

Just add some fruit and you've got breakfast.

2-1/2 c. biscuit baking mix
3/4 c. half-and-half
3 T. oil
1 egg, lightly beaten

3/4 c. diced ham
3/4 c. shredded sharp Cheddar
   cheese

Pour biscuit mix into a mixing bowl; make a well in center. Combine remaining ingredients; pour into well and stir just until moistened. Spoon into 12 greased muffin tins, filling two-thirds full. Bake at 400 degrees for 11 to 12 minutes or until toothpick inserted in center comes out clean. Makes one dozen.

Let's Pack
a Picnic Basket

Peanut Butter-Sunflower Sammies

Connie Bryant
Topeka, KS

So tasty that the children will never know they're healthy too.

1/2 c. creamy peanut butter	2 T. raisins
1/4 c. carrot, shredded	2 T. honey
2 T. sunflower kernels	8 slices whole-wheat bread

Combine all ingredients except bread in a bowl; mix well. Spread mixture on 4 bread slices; top each with remaining slices. Serves 4.

Keep a basket of picnic supplies in your car for picnics at a moment's notice! With a quilt or tablecloth, paper napkins, plates and cups you'll always be ready. Just pick up sandwich fixin's and drinks and you're ready to go!

Scrumptious Sandwich Loaves

Dee Ann Ice
Delaware, OH

You'll feed quite a crowd with these sandwiches...easy to make ahead too!

2 loaves Italian bread
8-oz. pkg. cream cheese, softened
1 c. shredded Cheddar cheese
3/4 c. green onion, chopped

1/4 c. mayonnaise
1 T. Worcestershire sauce
1 lb. sliced deli ham
1 lb. sliced roast beef
1/4 to 1/2 c. sliced dill pickles

Cut loaves in half lengthwise; hollow out halves. Set aside. Combine cheeses, onion, mayonnaise and Worcestershire sauce; spread over both halves of bread. Layer ham, beef and pickles on bottom halves of bread; press on top halves. Wrap in plastic wrap; refrigerate for at least 2 hours. Cut into 1-1/2 to 2-inch slices. Serves 12 to 14.

Safety first! Keep hot foods hot, cold foods cold, and don't let any picnic foods stand out longer than 2 hours...even if the food looks just fine.

Let's Pack a Picnic Basket

Hit-the-Road Sandwiches

Kay Marone
Des Moines, IA

*Make these yummy sandwiches the night before your picnic.
Pack 'em up the next day and you're ready to roll!*

2/3 c. shredded Cheddar cheese
1/2 c. deli ham, chopped
1 carrot, peeled and shredded
1 stalk celery, chopped
2 to 3 t. sweet pickle relish

1/3 c. sliced green olives
8-oz. container spreadable
   cream cheese with chives,
   softened
1 loaf sliced whole-wheat bread

Combine shredded cheese, ham, carrot, celery, pickle relish and olives in a bowl; mix well and set aside. Spread each slice of bread with cream cheese on one side and sprinkle with about 1/3 cup shredded cheese mixture. Top with another slice of bread. Trim off crusts, if desired; slice each sandwich into quarters. Wrap with plastic wrap and refrigerate several hours or overnight. Makes about 6.

America is not like a blanket...one piece of unbroken cloth,
the same color, the same texture, the same size.
America is more like a quilt...many pieces, many colors, many
sizes, all woven and held together by a common thread.

-Rev. Jesse Jackson

Muffuletta Sandwich

Kris Bailey
Conklin, NY

This is one of my family's favorites. Try it with different cold cuts and cheeses...great with salami, Swiss and provolone.

3/4 c. green olives, chopped
3/4 c. black olives, chopped
1 clove garlic, minced
1/3 c. pimento, chopped
1/4 c. fresh parsley, chopped
3/4 t. dried oregano
1/4 t. pepper
1/3 c. plus 1 T. olive oil, divided

1 round loaf Italian bread
1/2 lb. sliced honey ham
1/2 lb. sliced turkey
1/4 lb. sliced Muenster cheese
Optional: mayonnaise-style
   salad dressing
8 to 10 slices dill pickle

Mix olives, garlic, pimento, herbs, pepper and 1/3 cup oil in a small bowl; set aside. Cut loaf in half horizontally and hollow out the center. Brush cut side of bottom half with remaining oil; layer ham, turkey and cheese slices on top. If you like, spread salad dressing between the layers. Top with pickle slices. Fill top half of loaf with the olive mixture; place bottom loaf on top and invert. Wrap tightly in plastic wrap and refrigerate overnight. Let stand until loaf comes to room temperature; cut into wedges. Makes 6 to 8 servings.

Give your kids their own road maps when you travel...they can trace the route with markers and see how much farther you have to go.

Colossal Hero Sandwich

Kathy Unruh
Fresno, CA

A classic! To make cutting easy, just push long toothpicks into the sandwich, then cut between the toothpicks with a serrated knife.

1 loaf Italian bread
2 c. romaine lettuce, shredded
2 T. Italian salad dressing
1/4 t. dried oregano
1/2 lb. sliced salami
6-oz. pkg. sliced provolone
    cheese
1 to 2 tomatoes, thinly sliced

1/2 lb. sliced deli ham
7-oz. jar roasted red peppers,
    drained and patted dry
6 pepperoncini, sliced
2-1/4 oz. can sliced black olives,
    drained
1 red onion, thinly sliced

Slice loaf in half lengthwise. With a fork, carefully hollow out the center; fill hollow with lettuce. Combine dressing and oregano in a small bowl; mix well and drizzle over lettuce. Layer remaining ingredients over lettuce. Cover with top of loaf and slice into individual portions. Serves 6 to 8.

Packing a hot dish for a picnic or potluck? Keep it hot by wrapping the dish first in foil, then in several layers of newspaper.

Date & Pecan Chicken Salad

Linda Davidson
Grove City, OH

A tasty and different chicken salad, great on buttered raisin bread.

1 c. cooked chicken, diced
1/4 c. bacon, crisply cooked and
   crumbled
1/4 c. chopped dates

1/4 c. chopped pecans
1/2 c. mayonnaise
1/4 t. sugar

Combine all ingredients in a small bowl; mix well. Serves 4.

Fancy Chicken Salad

Andrea Miller
Sugar Land, TX

Delicious as either a sandwich filling or a salad.

2 c. cooked chicken, diced
1/2 c. celery, diced
1/3 c. seedless grapes, halved
2 green onions, sliced
1/3 c. slivered almonds

1/2 c. mayonnaise
1/2 t. Worcestershire sauce
1/2 t. curry powder
salt and pepper to taste

Combine chicken, celery, grapes, onions and almonds. Blend in mayonnaise, Worcestershire sauce and curry powder; add salt and pepper to taste. Serves 4 to 6.

Freeze juice boxes or bottles when packing a cooler...they'll be cool to drink when you're ready and help keep your other foods cold.

Ladybugs on a Branch

Jen Sell
Farmington, MN

Kids really enjoy making and eating this fun treat!

1/2 c. peanut butter
2 T. honey
3 stalks celery, cut into 3-inch
    lengths

1/4 c. sweetened, dried
    cranberries

Blend peanut butter and honey in a small bowl until smooth. Spread celery with mixture; arrange cranberries on top. Makes 9.

Let the kids choose their own picture postcards on family trips...punch 2 holes on the side and tie with ribbon to make a little book. Have them sign and date the cards, then add their comments about each site...fun mementos!

Grandma Jean's Tuna Spread

Wendy Lee Paffenroth
Pine Island, NY

My family loves this on a hard roll with tomato and lettuce. It's excellent as a spread for crackers or a vegetable dip too.

2 6-oz. cans tuna, drained
8-oz. pkg. light cream cheese
1/2 c. light mayonnaise
1/2 t. pepper
1/2 t. hot pepper sauce

1/2 t. dried chives
1 t. dried parsley
2 T. onion, minced
Garnish: paprika, sliced olives

In a small mixing bowl, blend all ingredients with a hand mixer. Refrigerate until ready to serve. Sprinkle with paprika and decorate with olive slices. Makes about 3 cups.

Crunchy Tuna Roll-Ups

Sherry Gordon
Arlington Heights, IL

Another easy-to-pack sandwich for your picnic basket.

2 6-oz. cans tuna, drained
1/2 c. sliced water chestnuts, chopped
1/2 c. green onion, chopped
1/3 c. red pepper, chopped

Optional: 4 eggs, hard-boiled, peeled and chopped
1/2 c. mayonnaise
4 8-inch flour tortillas
2 c. romaine lettuce, shredded

Combine all ingredients except tortillas and lettuce; spread on tortillas. Sprinkle with lettuce and roll up each tortilla tightly. Slice in half diagonally; wrap in plastic wrap and refrigerate up to 3 hours. Makes 8 servings.

Let's Pack
a Picnic Basket

Mark's Egg Salad Sandwiches

Connie Herek
Bay City, MI

I must confess...this is my husband's recipe. It's so delicious!

6 eggs, hard-boiled, peeled and
  chopped
1/3 c. celery, finely chopped
1/3 c. onion, finely chopped
3 to 4 T. mayonnaise-style salad
  dressing
1 to 2 t. mustard

1 t. Worcestershire sauce
1/2 t. salt
1/4 t. pepper
1/2 t. dry mustard
1 T. dill weed
1 loaf sliced bread

Mix all ingredients except bread in a small bowl; refrigerate for about one hour. Spread on bread. Makes about 6 to 8 servings.

Bring extra Frisbees® to your next picnic...they make great paper plate holders at lunch and are fun for the kids afterwards!

Country-Fried Chicken

Dolores Brock
Prescott Valley, AZ

*Delicious served hot with fluffy biscuits, gravy & mashed potatoes...a
"must" for picnics served cold with potato salad!*

1 c. all-purpose flour
1 t. salt
1 t. pepper
1 t. garlic salt
1 t. poultry seasoning

1 c. milk
1 egg, beaten
3 to 4 lbs. chicken
2 c. oil

Mix together flour, salt, pepper, garlic salt and poultry seasoning in
a bowl; set aside. Blend together milk and egg in another bowl. Dip
chicken in milk mixture; coat with flour mixture. Heat oil in a large
skillet; fry chicken pieces until golden on both sides. Lower heat and
simmer for an additional 20 to 30 minutes, until chicken is cooked
through. Serves 4 to 6.

Serve fried chicken in clean new paper buckets from the
local paint store. Lined with red-checked paper napkins
just for fun, they're easy to toss when the picnic is over!

Hearty Meatloaf Sandwiches

Nancy Wise
Little Rock, AR

Why wait for leftover meatloaf to enjoy these sandwiches?

1-1/2 lbs. ground beef
1/2 lb. ground pork
1 c. quick-cooking oats,
   uncooked
1/2 c. dry Italian bread crumbs
1/2 c. onion, chopped
1/2 c. celery, chopped
1/2 c. green pepper, chopped

8-oz. can tomato sauce
1 egg
1/2 t. salt
1/4 t. pepper
1/4 c. catsup
1 loaf sourdough bread, sliced
Garnish: mayonnaise, sliced
   tomato, lettuce leaves

Combine beef and pork in a large bowl; make a well in the center.
Add remaining ingredients except catsup and bread. Use your hands to
mix ingredients together evenly. Form into a loaf and place in a
greased 8"x4" loaf pan. Bake at 350 degrees for 45 minutes; spread
catsup on top, return to oven and bake an additional 15 to
20 minutes. Let stand for 15 minutes; remove from pan. Serve hot or
cold, sliced and placed on bread with mayonnaise, tomato and lettuce
to taste. Makes about 6 servings.

Take a vacation trip in your hometown! Check out all
the places you've always meant to go...gardens, craft shops,
historic houses. Pack a picnic lunch and stop at a park you've
never visited before. A great getaway when you have
a free day.

Hoagie Dip

Kelly Alderson
Erie, PA

Even easier than sandwiches...simply pack a tub of dip and a bag of fresh bread cubes.

1/2 lb. salami, thinly sliced
1/2 lb. deli ham, thinly sliced
1 lb. sliced American cheese
2 c. mayonnaise
1 to 2 T. red wine vinegar
2 t. dried oregano

3/4 c. tomato, chopped
Optional: 1/2 c. onion, diced
2 tomatoes, diced
2 c. shredded lettuce
Italian bread, cubed

Chop salami, ham and cheese into small pieces; place in a mixing bowl and set aside. Blend together mayonnaise, vinegar and oregano; mix into salami mixture until well coated. Stir in onion, if using; chill. At serving time, mix in tomatoes and lettuce. Serve with cubed Italian bread for dipping. Makes about 8 cups.

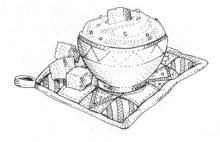

BLT Dip

Tammy Carnaghi
Westerville, IL

A hollowed-out head of lettuce makes a clever serving bowl.

16-oz. pkg. bacon, crisply
　cooked and crumbled
1 tomato, chopped
1/2 c. onion, chopped

2 c. mayonnaise-type salad
　dressing
bread, cubed

Combine all ingredients except bread; mix well and chill. Serve with cubed or sliced bread for dipping. Makes about 4 cups.

Vickie's Gazpacho Dip

Vickie

Fresh summer flavors in a dip that's great with tortilla chips!

3 tomatoes, diced
3 avocados, diced
4 green onions, thinly sliced
4-oz. can diced green chiles
3 T. olive oil

1-1/2 T. cider vinegar
1 t. garlic salt
1 t. salt
1/4 t. pepper

Combine tomatoes, avocados, onions and chiles in a large bowl; set aside. Combine remaining ingredients; drizzle over vegetables and toss gently. Cover and chill. Makes about 6 cups.

What's your hurry? Take the road less traveled on your next family trip...you'll see farmstands, charming small towns and scenic views that you might miss otherwise.

Herb Garden Dip

Kendall Hale
Lynn, MA

For a lighter dip, try replacing some of the sour cream with non-fat plain yogurt or fat-free mayonnaise.

1 c. sour cream
1/2 t. dried chives
1/2 t. dried parsley
1/2 t. dried marjoram
1/4 t. garlic powder

1/4 t. dried oregano
1/4 t. dried basil
1/8 t. dill weed
chips or crackers
assorted vegetables for dipping

Place sour cream in a small bowl and set aside. Crush together herbs; stir into sour cream and chill well. Serve with snack chips and fresh vegetables. Makes about one cup.

Crispy Parmesan Pita Crackers

Laura Fuller
Fort Wayne, IN

Great with salads and dips! For added flavor, sprinkle with garlic powder or dried herbs before baking.

6 pita rounds

grated Parmesan cheese

Split pitas and cut each half into 6 wedges. Arrange on a baking sheet; spray lightly with non-stick vegetable spray and sprinkle with grated Parmesan. Bake at 350 degrees for 10 minutes or until crisp. Makes about 6 dozen.

Let's Pack
a Picnic Basket

Kiddies' Favorite Trail Mix

Marian Buckley
Fontana, CA

*Pack in snack-size plastic zipping bags...handy for
quieting cries of "Are we there yet?"*

4 c. bite-size crispy corn cereal
   squares
1 c. peanuts

1 c. raisins
1/2 c. dried bananas, chopped
1 c. candy-coated chocolates

Combine all ingredients in a large covered container; mix well. Makes
about 7-1/2 cups.

New plastic pails make whimsical picnic servers for chips and
snacks. After lunch, the kids can use them for treasure
hunting around the picnic grounds.

Tomato-Bacon Nibbles

Anna McMaster
Portland, OR

A 1/4-teaspoon measuring spoon is just right for
scooping out tiny tomatoes for stuffing.

24 to 30 cherry tomatoes
16-oz. pkg. bacon, cooked and
   crisply crumbled
2 T. fresh parsley, chopped

1/2 c. green onion, finely
   chopped
3 T. grated Parmesan cheese
1/2 c. mayonnaise

Cut a thin slice off the top of each tomato; scoop out and discard
tomato pulp. Place tomatoes upside-down on a paper towel to drain
for 30 minutes. Mix remaining ingredients in a small bowl; stuff
tomatoes. Chill several hours or overnight. Makes 2 to 2-1/2 dozen.

It's a challenge to keep foods chilled on
a hot, sunny day when everyone is opening and closing
the cooler to get cold drinks. Make it easy...pack one
cooler with beverages and another
with meats, salads and other perishable foods.

Let's Pack
a Picnic Basket

Classic Deviled Eggs

Karen Norman
Jacksonville, FL

Seems like people can never get enough of these! For picnics, pair eggs and wrap in plastic film.

1 doz. eggs, hard-boiled, peeled
   and halved lengthwise
1/2 c. mayonnaise
2-1/2 T. sweet pickle relish

1 t. mustard
1/4 t. salt
1/8 t. pepper
Garnish: paprika

Separate hard-boiled egg yolks from egg whites; arrange egg whites on a serving plate and set aside. Mash egg yolks in a bowl; combine with remaining ingredients except paprika and mix well. Fill egg whites with mixture; sprinkle with paprika. Makes 2 dozen.

Scottish Eggs

Brenda Tucker
Saint Helens, OR

So easy to pack...so tasty to eat!

2 lbs. ground sausage
1 doz. eggs, hard-boiled and
   peeled

2 c. dry Italian bread crumbs

Divide sausage into 12 portions. Flatten each portion and wrap it around an egg to completely cover the egg. Repeat with remaining sausage and eggs. Roll eggs in bread crumbs; arrange in a baking pan and bake at 425 degrees for about 1-1/2 hours. Serve warm or cold, cut into halves or quarters. Makes 2 to 4 dozen.

Eggs won't crack during boiling if you add a tablespoon or 2 of white vinegar to the water.

Tangy Tomato Slices

Jennifer Eveland-Kupp
Temple, PA

Is there anything more scrumptious than a ripe tomato?

6 tomatoes, thinly sliced
1 onion, thinly sliced
1 c. oil
1/3 c. vinegar
1/4 c. fresh parsley, chopped
3 T. fresh basil, chopped

1 T. sugar
1 t. salt
1/2 t. pepper
1/2 t. dry mustard
1/2 t. garlic powder

Layer tomato and onion slices in a 13"x9" baking dish; set aside.
Combine oil, vinegar and seasonings in a small bowl; mix well and
pour over tomatoes. Cover and chill 4 to 5 hours. Serves 6 to 8.

A vintage wooden soft-drink crate makes a handy carrier for
condiments, drinks and all the things we need for a picnic!

Let's Pack
a Picnic Basket

Peppy 4-Bean Salad

Debi DeVore
Dover, OH

This is my mom's recipe...we enjoy it at all our family cookouts.

14-1/2 oz. can green beans,
    drained
14-1/2 oz. can yellow beans,
    drained
15-1/2 oz. can kidney beans,
    drained
16-oz. can lima beans, drained
14-1/2 oz. can sliced carrots,
    drained

1 green pepper, chopped
1 red onion, chopped
1 c. celery, chopped
1/2 c. vinegar
1/2 c. water
1/2 c. oil
2 c. sugar
1 t. celery seed
1 t. salt

Mix together all the vegetables in a large bowl; set aside. Combine remaining ingredients; toss with bean mixture. Cover and refrigerate for at least 24 hours. Makes 10 to 12 servings.

Colorful bandannas make great picnic napkins...look for inexpensive ones in all kinds of fun prints at your local craft store.

Best-Ever Potato Salad

Cindy Blauser
Mohnton, PA

*An egg slicer makes it easy to chop hard-boiled eggs for potato salad.
Just slice the egg, then turn it a quarter turn and slice again.*

4 c. redskin potatoes, cubed
14-1/2 oz. can chicken broth
1 T. cider vinegar
1/2 c. carrots, peeled and
    chopped

3/4 c. celery, chopped
2 eggs, hard-boiled, peeled and
    chopped
1 T. dill weed

Combine potatoes and broth in a saucepan; bring to a boil. Lower
heat, cover and simmer for about 10 minutes or until tender. Drain
and place in a bowl; mix in remaining ingredients. Toss with dressing;
chill before serving. Serves 8.

Dressing:

1/2 c. mayonnaise
1 T. Dijon mustard
1 T. sweet pickle relish

1/4 t. salt
1/4 t. pepper

Mix all ingredients together.

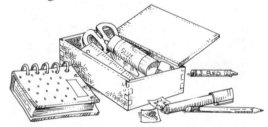

Pack blank books, markers, scissors and glue sticks so the kids
can make their own travel journals. Encourage them to add
stickers, ticket stubs, clippings and tiny trinkets. They'll
amuse themselves and you'll see the trip through their eyes.

Let's Pack a Picnic Basket

Mashed Potato Salad

Lisa Colombo
Appleton, WI

This is a great summer dish...it's a hit with all our friends.

5 lbs. potatoes, peeled and
   boiled
1-1/2 c. mayonnaise-type salad
   dressing
1 T. mustard
salt and pepper to taste

2 eggs, hard-boiled, peeled
   and chopped
1 c. onion, chopped
1/2 c. green pepper, chopped
1/2 c. red pepper, chopped
1/2 c. cucumber, chopped

Mash potatoes in a large mixing bowl. Fold in salad dressing, mustard, salt and pepper. Add remaining ingredients; mix well. Chill before serving. Serves 8 to 10.

Watch for unusual road signs along the way...what fun to take family snapshots in front of signs for the World's Biggest Tire or Mystery Hill!

7-Layer Overnight Salad

Marie Needham
Columbus, OH

A favorite at potlucks! Easy to increase for a larger crowd...just add a little more of everything.

1 head lettuce, torn into bite-size pieces
1 to 2 onions, thinly sliced and separated into rings
10-oz. pkg. frozen peas
3 to 4 eggs, hard-boiled, peeled and sliced
4-oz. jar bacon bits
8-oz. jar mayonnaise
1-1/2 c. grated Parmesan cheese

Arrange 1/3 of lettuce in a large bowl. Top with 1/3 each of the onions, frozen peas, eggs and bacon bits. Repeat layering twice. Spoon mayonnaise completely over top; sprinkle with Parmesan. Cover and refrigerate overnight. Makes 8 to 10 servings.

Iceberg & Thousand Island Salad

April Jacobs
Loveland, CO

An all-time salad classic.

1 c. mayonnaise
1/3 c. chili sauce
1 T. green olives, chopped
1 T. pimento, chopped
1 egg, hard-boiled, peeled and divided
1 head lettuce, cut into 6 wedges

Combine mayonnaise, chili sauce, olives and pimento in a jar. Chop egg yolk and add to mixture, reserving egg white for another recipe. Blend well; chill. To serve, arrange lettuce wedges on individual plates; divide dressing among the wedges. Serves 6.

Creamy Garden Coleslaw

Jackie Crough
Salina, KS

Save time by picking up a package of shredded coleslaw mix.

1 head cabbage, shredded
1 zucchini, shredded
1 c. carrots, peeled and grated
1/2 c. green pepper, chopped
3/4 c. mayonnaise

2 T. sugar
2 t. lemon juice
1 t. celery seed
1/2 t. salt

Combine all ingredients in a large bowl; toss lightly. Cover and chill for about 15 to 20 minutes. Serves 12.

Packing a tossed salad? Put the dressing in the bottom of your container, topped with greens and veggies. At mealtime, just stir or shake for a crisp salad every time!

Pineapple Gelatin in a Can

Linda Behling
Cecil, PA

This is a very pretty dessert, and it's made right in the can! The kids get a kick out of making this…and it's so easy to pack for a picnic.

20-oz. can pineapple slices
3-oz. pkg. favorite-flavor
　gelatin mix

1 c. boiling water
Garnish: lettuce leaves

Drain pineapple, but leave the slices in the can. Dissolve gelatin in boiling water in a small bowl; pour into the can, over the pineapple. Chill for 2-1/2 hours or overnight until set. To serve, run a knife around the inside of the can and slide it out. Slice between pineapple slices and arrange on lettuce leaves. Serves 5 to 6.

Sprinkle baking soda in your picnic cooler
each time you put it away…it'll be fresh and sweet
the next time you use it.

Let's Pack
a Picnic Basket

Pineapple Picnic Salad

Michelle Campen
Peoria, IL

Everyone loves this creamy, tangy delight!

20-oz. can crushed pineapple
8-oz. pkg. cream cheese,
   softened
3-1/2 oz. pkg. instant vanilla
   pudding mix

20-oz. can pineapple chunks,
   drained
8-oz. container frozen whipped
   topping, thawed

Combine crushed pineapple and juice with cream cheese in a large
serving bowl; stir in pudding mix. Fold in pineapple chunks and
whipped topping. Cover and refrigerate until ready to serve. Makes
10 to 12 servings.

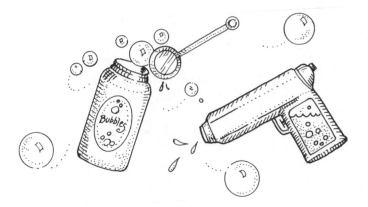

Bring along bubble wands, jump ropes and squirt guns
to your next outing...grownups will have as much fun as
kids and you'll be able to take some great
candid snapshots.

Orange-Pineapple Salad

Jacquelynn Daunce
Lockport, NY

When I was a kid, traveling to my best friend's cottage in Canada was a real treat. A warm sandy beach, a bonfire, hot dogs and Mrs. Y's gelatin salad...memories in the making!

3 3-oz. pkgs. orange gelatin
    mix
3/4 c. sugar
20-oz. can crushed pineapple
3 c. cold water
1 c. chopped nuts
8-oz. container frozen whipped
    topping, thawed
Optional: lettuce leaves

Combine gelatin, sugar and pineapple with juice in a saucepan; boil for 3 minutes. Remove from heat; stir in cold water. Pour into an 8"x8" glass dish. Chill for 20 minutes until mixture is at room temperature and partially set; fold in nuts and whipped topping. Blend well and chill an additional 20 minutes until set. Cut into squares and serve as a salad on lettuce leaves or as a dessert. Makes 6 to 8 servings.

Traveling a distance to your cookout site? Wrap and freeze burgers or marinated meat before packing in your ice chest. The frozen meat will help keep other items cold and will thaw in time for grilling.

Lemon-Lime Gooseberry Salad

Judy Borecky
Escondido, CA

Four generations of our family have lived here in California, but this salad reminds us of our relatives back in Kansas where gooseberries grow.

15-oz. can gooseberries
1/2 c. sugar
3-oz. pkg. lemon gelatin mix
3-oz. pkg. lime gelatin mix
2 c. boiling water

1/2 t. lemon extract
1 c. celery, diced
1/2 c. chopped pecans
1 c. shredded Cheddar cheese

Combine gooseberries and their syrup with sugar in a medium saucepan; heat and stir until sugar dissolves. Bring just to a boil over medium heat. Let cool. Dissolve gelatin mixes in water in a large bowl; cool. Add lemon extract. Combine gooseberry mixture with gelatin mixture; blend well. Fold in celery, nuts and cheese. Pour into an 11"x7" glass dish. Chill until set, at least 3 hours. Cut into squares to serve; drizzle with dressing. Serves 8 to 10.

Dressing:

1/2 c. mayonnaise
1 T. honey

3 T. French salad dressing

Whisk together ingredients in a small bowl.

Pack a scout-style pocketknife with can opener, corkscrew and other utensils in your picnic kit...so handy!

Potluck Pasta Salad

Joy Diomede
Double Oak, TX

Try it with other veggies like yellow squash or peas.

12-oz. pkg. rainbow rotini pasta, uncooked
16-oz. bottle zesty Italian salad dressing
1 t. red pepper flakes
2-1/2 oz. can sliced black olives, drained
3-oz. jar sliced green olives, drained
4 oz. smoked Cheddar cheese, cubed
4 oz. Pepper Jack cheese, cubed
4 oz. pepperoni, cubed
4 oz. salami, cubed
1/2 c. green onion, sliced
6-oz. can smoked almonds

Cook pasta according to package directions; drain and rinse with cold water. Place in a large salad bowl; cool to room temperature. Stir in all ingredients except almonds, cover and refrigerate at least 2 hours. Stir in almonds at serving time. Makes 6 to 8 servings.

Give your kids a disposable camera to record reunion events...their snapshots may be off-center, but you'll see the world from their eyes!

Let's Pack a Picnic Basket

Grandma's Macaroni Salad

Mary Modig
Sturbridge, MA

My brother and I took turns spending time at Grandma & Grandpa's house during summer vacation. Grandma always fixed my favorite macaroni salad for me.

8-oz. pkg. elbow macaroni,
   cooked
1 egg, hard-boiled, peeled and
   chopped
1 carrot, peeled and grated
1 tomato, chopped
1 onion, chopped
2 stalks celery, chopped

1 green pepper, chopped
1 t. salt
pepper to taste
fresh parsley to taste, chopped
5 T. mayonnaise
3 T. vinegar
3 T. olive oil
Garnish: paprika

Combine macaroni, egg, carrot, tomato, onion, celery, green pepper, salt, pepper and parsley in a large bowl; set aside. Mix remaining ingredients together in a small bowl; toss with macaroni mixture. Refrigerate until chilled; sprinkle with paprika. Serves 6 to 8.

What is a family, after all, except memories? Haphazard and precious as the contents of a catch-all drawer in the kitchen.

-Joyce Carol Oates

Old-Fashioned Lemonade

Jessica Parker
Mulvane, KS

Lemons will yield lots more juice if you roll them back and forth on the countertop before juicing.

juice of 6 lemons
1 c. sugar

6 c. cold water

Stir together all ingredients in a one-gallon pitcher. Adjust sweetness to taste with additional water or sugar. Chill and serve over ice. Makes 6 servings.

Meadow Tea

Susan Eckert
Palmyra, PA

I remember my mother making pitchers of this tasty Pennsylvania Dutch concoction in the summertime. I like to freeze the concentrate in one-cup containers to enjoy all year long.

2 c. fresh mint leaves, washed
    and packed
2 to 2-1/2 c. sugar

4 c. water
Garnish: fresh mint

Place all ingredients in a medium stockpot. Boil for 5 minutes; turn off heat and let stand for 5 hours. Strain through a coffee filter-lined sieve, squeezing excess liquid from mint leaves. To serve, add one cup concentrate to 2 quarts cold water in a pitcher. Serve with ice and a garnish of mint. Makes 4 cups concentrate; about 8 servings per one cup concentrate.

Let's Pack
a Picnic Basket

Ginger Sun Tea

Michelle Campen
Peoria, IL

A refreshing beverage that's just a little different.

4-1/2 c. cold water
8 teabags
1 to 2-inch slice fresh ginger,
   peeled and thinly sliced

2 to 4 T. sugar
2 12-oz. bottles ginger ale,
   chilled
Garnish: orange slices

Combine water, teabags and ginger in a 2-quart glass container; cover with a lid or plastic wrap. Let stand in full sun or at room temperature for 2 to 3 hours. Remove teabags; stir in sugar. Cover and chill. At serving time, strain into a 2-quart pitcher. Stir in ginger ale, pour over ice and garnish with orange slices. Makes 8 servings.

Homemade Root Beer

Robin Luengas
Sugar Land, TX

This recipe is a family tradition...we make it every 4th of July.

1 gal. water
2 c. sugar

2 T. root beer extract
2 lbs. dry ice

Use a plastic spoon to mix water, sugar and extract together in a 2-gallon plastic cooler or other wide-mouth plastic container. Wearing gloves to protect hands, carefully add dry ice. Let stand 20 minutes until dry ice has evaporated. Makes one gallon.

Chocolate Picnic Cake

Jo Anne Hayon
Sheboygan, WI

*My mother always made this cake for special occasions or to treat us.
My sisters and I used to enjoy picking the chocolate chips out of the
baked cake, hoping she wouldn't catch us!*

18-1/2 oz. chocolate cake mix   6-oz. pkg. chocolate chips
1 T. all-purpose flour   Garnish: powdered sugar

Mix cake according to package directions; stir in flour and pour into
a greased 13"x9" baking pan. Sprinkle with chocolate chips; bake
according to package directions. Let cool in pan; when cooled, sprinkle
with powdered sugar. Cut into squares. Makes 12 to 15 servings.

Bake up some cookie bars, then cut, wrap and freeze
individually. Later you can pull out just what you need for
a last-minute picnic.

Brittany's Cheesecake Brownies

Paula Friedel
Taneytown, MD

My niece loves these microwave brownies so much that I've named them for her. They are always a hit wherever we take them!

5 T. butter
2 1-oz. sqs. unsweetened
    chocolate
1-1/4 c. sugar, divided
3 eggs, divided
2 t. vanilla extract, divided

2/3 c. all-purpose flour
1 t. baking powder
8-oz. pkg. cream cheese
6-oz. pkg. semi-sweet chocolate
    chips
Optional: 1/2 c. chopped walnuts

Combine butter and chocolate in a large microwave-safe bowl. Cover and microwave on high for one to 2 minutes; stir until smooth. Beat in 2/3 cup sugar, 2 eggs and one teaspoon vanilla. Add flour and baking powder; stir until blended. Spread in a greased microwave-safe 8"x8" baking pan; set aside. Place cream cheese in a microwave-safe bowl. Heat on high for 45 seconds to one minute until soft; stir until smooth. Beat in remaining sugar, egg and vanilla; spoon over chocolate mixture and cut through with knife to swirl. Sprinkle with chocolate chips and nuts, if desired. Shield corners of pan with small triangles of aluminum foil. Place pan on an inverted plate in microwave oven. Heat, uncovered, at 70% power for 11 to 13 minutes or until a toothpick comes out clean; rotate a half turn after 5 minutes. Heat on high one minute. Cool on a wire rack; cut into squares. Store in refrigerator. Makes one dozen.

Let the kids make their own picnic sandwiches...after all, you're outdoors and so is the mess! You'll enjoy the pride they take in their creations.

Dorothy's Raisin Bars

Delinda Blakney
Dallas, GA

This is one of my mom's favorite recipes.

1 c. raisins
3/4 c. apple juice
2 T. shortening
1 c. all-purpose flour
1/2 t. salt
1/2 t. baking soda

1/2 t. baking powder
1 t. cinnamon
1/4 t. ground cloves
1/8 t. nutmeg
Optional: 1/4 c. chopped nuts

In a small saucepan, bring raisins, apple juice and shortening to a boil. Remove from heat and cool. Mix remaining ingredients in a bowl; stir into raisin mixture. Pour into a greased 8"x8" baking pan. Bake at 350 degrees for 35 to 40 minutes; remove from oven and cool. Cut into 2-inch squares; store in tightly covered container. Makes 16.

Don't forget a pail so kids can collect seashells at the beach or pine cones and rocks in the woods. Back home, set the kids down with craft glue, wiggly eyes and pipe cleaners...they can turn their "finds" into funny creatures!

Bestus Banana Bars

Judy Taylor
Butler, MO

My Aunt Irene gave me the recipe for these bars, and my 4-year-old twin grandsons love them. One of them came to me and said, "Grandma, this is the BESTUS cake I have ever eaten." It makes me smile just to remember how sweet he sounded!

1-1/2 c. sugar
1/2 c. butter, softened
2 eggs, beaten
1 c. sour cream
3 bananas, mashed
2 t. vanilla extract

2 c. all-purpose flour
1 t. baking soda
1 t. salt
1-1/2 c. pecans, finely chopped
   and divided

Blend together sugar and butter until fluffy. Add eggs and sour cream, blending well. Mix in bananas and vanilla. Sift together flour, baking soda and salt; add to mixture. Stir until completely mixed. Add one cup pecans. Spread in a greased, floured jelly-roll pan. Bake for 20 to 25 minutes at 350 degrees. Frost when cooled; sprinkle with remaining pecans and cut into 3"x1" bars. Makes about 3-1/2 dozen.

Frosting:

3-oz. pkg. cream cheese,
   softened
2 t. butter, softened

2 c. powdered sugar
milk

Blend together cream cheese and butter; add powdered sugar. Stir in milk to make a spreading consistency.

PB Sandwich Cookies

Chris Sutherland
Eastpointe, MI

My Grandmother Ann taught my dad this recipe. One day he made a batch with my 2-year-old daughter, Victoria. It took me 45 minutes to scrape the peanut butter off everything in my kitchen, including my dad and my daughter...they laughed and laughed! I am so glad that my dad is keeping my grandmother's legacy alive.

16-oz. pkg. powdered sugar
1 c. milk

28-oz. jar creamy peanut butter
16-oz. pkg. graham crackers

Mix together the powdered sugar and milk in a bowl. Add three-fourths of the peanut butter; mix well. Add more peanut butter if necessary to make a pasty consistency. Spread mixture on half of a graham cracker and top with the other half, making a sandwich. The number of cookies made will depend on how much you spread on each cracker.

On a clear sunny day, what fun to lie on the grass and watch fluffy clouds for hidden shapes! At night, out in the country, watch for shooting stars, maybe even the Milky Way!

Pecan Chews

Ann Cass
Danielsville, GA

No self-rising flour in the cupboard? Just replace the 2 cups of self-rising flour with 2 cups all-purpose flour plus one tablespoon baking powder and 1/4 teaspoon salt.

16-oz. pkg. brown sugar
1/2 c. margarine, softened
4 eggs, beaten

2 c. self-rising flour
2 c. chopped pecans

Combine brown sugar and margarine in top of a double boiler; stir in the eggs. Heat over boiling water for 20 minutes, stirring constantly. Add flour and pecans; mix well. Pour batter into a greased 13"x9" baking pan. Bake at 325 degrees for 30 minutes. Cut into bars and remove from pan immediately. Makes 2-1/2 to 3 dozen.

Make a trip bag for each of your kids...a special tote bag or backpack that's filled with favorite small toys and fun stuff, reserved just for road trips. The miles will go by much faster!

Lunchbox Cake

Dawn Menard
Seekonk, MA

This is my brother's favorite...perfect for packing in a lunchbox.

2-1/4 c. all-purpose flour
2 t. baking soda
1 t. salt
1 c. brown sugar, packed
2 eggs

1/4 c. butter, softened
16-oz. can fruit cocktail
1/2 c. chopped walnuts
1/2 c. chocolate chips

Combine all ingredients except nuts and chips in a large bowl. Mix with a hand mixer on medium setting for 2 minutes. Pour into a greased, floured 13"x9" baking pan; sprinkle nuts and chips on top. Bake at 350 degrees for 35 to 40 minutes, until center springs back to the touch. Let cool; cut into squares. Makes one to 1-1/2 dozen.

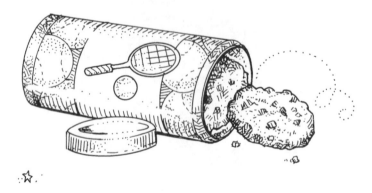

Save empty tennis ball tubes...they're perfect for carrying stacks of cookies to picnics.

Cale's Corn Flake Cookies

Lori Hobscheidt
Washington, IA

Sweet, crunchy and peanut buttery.

1 c. light corn syrup
1 c. creamy peanut butter
1 c. sugar

1 t. vanilla extract
6 to 7 c. corn flake cereal

Combine all ingredients except cereal in a heavy saucepan; heat and stir over low heat. Add cereal; stir well and drop by teaspoonfuls onto wax paper. Let stand until set. Makes 2 dozen.

No longer using Grandma's picnic basket? Fill it with potted flowers and display in a sunny room for a daily reminder of good times together.

Cherry-Coconut Bars

Becky Hall
Carthage, MO

Equally tasty with an icy glass of milk or a cup of hot tea!

1/2 c. butter, softened
3 T. powdered sugar
1-1/4 c. all-purpose flour,
    divided
2 eggs, beaten

1/2 c. flaked coconut
3/4 c. dried cherries
1/2 t. baking powder
1/4 t. salt
1 t. vanilla extract

Combine butter, sugar and one cup flour; pat into an ungreased 8"x8" baking pan. Bake at 350 degrees for 20 minutes or until golden. Mix remaining ingredients together; pour over hot crust. Bake for an additional 20 minutes; cool. Cut into bars. Makes 2 dozen.

A rectangular cake pan with its own lid makes a great lap tray for kids in the car...fill it with crayons, paper and small treats.

Honeybee Puddings

Kristi Hobson
Grapeland, TX

This dessert is fun to make for a picnic! Prepare in small covered bowls to pack in your cooler.

1 c. milk
3 T. honey
Optional: 2 to 3 drops yellow
    food coloring
3.4-oz. pkg. instant vanilla
    pudding
2 c. frozen whipped topping,
    thawed

1 c. chocolate wafer cookie
    crumbs, divided
6 chocolate wafer cookies,
    halved
6 black gumdrops
red or black string licorice

Combine milk, honey and food coloring in a bowl; add pudding mix and beat with a whisk for one to 2 minutes. Stir in whipped topping. Layer pudding mixture alternately with 3/4 cup cookie crumbs among 6 small, clear dessert dishes; refrigerate for one hour. Arrange 2 cookie halves on top of mixture in each dish to form wings. Decorate each with a gumdrop for the head; insert small pieces of licorice to form antennae and stinger. Sprinkle with reserved cookie crumbs between the wafer halves to form the body. Makes 6 servings.

Cut cheese slices into simple stars, flowers or other fun shapes for a playful addition to relish trays.

Grandma's Recipe Box

A special cookbook

Make color copies of Grandma's favorite recipe cards or cookbook pages complete with handwritten notes and smudges. Add sweet stories and photos. Dress up with patterned papers, decorative-edged scissors and a comb binding from a copy shop. Make enough copies for everyone, including the grandkids!

☆

Shadow box

Frame a special cookie recipe, a photo of Grandma and her special cookie cutter or a "cookie" made from salt dough or oven-drying clay, iced with puff paint. Use a color copy of her favorite tea towel for a pretty mat.

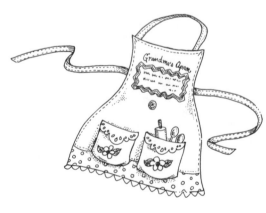

☆

Apron

Make a photo transfer of a recipe and iron onto a ready-made canvas apron. Trim with rick-rack, appliqués or buttons from Grandma's sewing basket.

Memory Boxes

The Family's Box of Postcards & Photographs

Frame
Frame postcards and photos in groups, adding small mementos, cut-outs and clips from snapshots.

Reunion T-shirts
Enlarge a "large letter" postcard with your hometown's name on a color copier, then add your family's name and reunion date below the picture. Make iron-on transfers and iron onto T-shirts for everyone at your reunion.

Pillows
Enlarge postcards and snapshots onto fabric transfers and stitch or glue to ready-made pillows. Add fringe or trim all around for a fun finishing touch.

A Joy Box

Rai Lynn Machin
Longview, TX

My young daughter, Payton, and I keep a Joy Box. It's a place for special keepsakes and accomplishments…an A+ on a school paper, pictures, letters from family & friends, thank you's saying how much somebody appreciates you, favorite verses, pretty rocks, etc. Then when one of us is blue and sad, we can go to the Joy Box and end our "pity party" by looking at all of the things that make us happy. There is always plenty in our Joy Box to make us smile! We have given Joy Boxes to many people as gifts, and we always put in a special item that we treasure to start them out, usually a picture or a piece of artwork drawn by my precious girl. We always attach a card that says, *"May your Joy Box always be full!"*

Copy, color and cut out this label, then have fun filling
a Joy Box for yourself or a special friend.

A Visit to the Farmers' Market

for you

Fresh fruit & veggie dishes

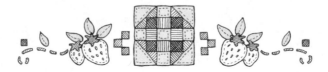

No-Cook Strawberry Freezer Jam

Dianne Gregory
Sheridan, AR

It's so simple to preserve the sunny taste of fresh strawberries!

7 c. strawberries, hulled
1-3/4 oz. pkg. light powdered
   pectin
1-3/4 c. sugar, divided

1 c. light corn syrup
8 1/2-pint freezer-safe plastic
   containers, sterilized

Thoroughly crush strawberries in a large bowl; set aside. Combine pectin with 1/4 cup sugar. Gradually add pectin mixture to strawberries, stirring vigorously. Let stand for 30 minutes, stirring occasionally. Add corn syrup; mix well. Gradually stir in remaining sugar until dissolved. Spoon into containers leaving 1/2-inch headspace; secure lids. Let stand overnight at room temperature before freezing. May be frozen up to one year. Store in refrigerator up to 4 weeks after opening. Makes 8 containers.

Lo-Cal Strawberry Freezer Jam

Melanie Lowe
Dover, DE

This jam is easy to make and has just 5 calories per tablespoon...what could be better?

4 c. strawberries, hulled
3 to 4 t. liquid artificial
   sweetener
1-3/4 oz. pkg. powdered pectin

1 T. lemon juice
4 to 5 1/2-pint canning jars
   and lids, sterilized

Crush strawberries in a medium saucepan. Stir in sweetener, pectin and lemon juice. Bring to a boil; boil for one minute. Remove from heat; stir for 2 minutes. Spoon into containers leaving 1/2-inch headspace; secure lids and freeze. Thaw before serving. Store in refrigerator up to 4 weeks after opening. Makes 4 to 5 jars.

A Visit to the Farmers' Market

Peachy Microwave Jam

Doris Billig
Gibbstown, NJ

This recipe is fast and easy! It's good over cake, ice cream and cereal...of course, it tastes scrumptious on bread too.

3 peaches, peeled, halved, pitted
   and chopped
1/2 c. sugar
2 T. honey

1 t. lemon juice
2 to 3 1/2-pint canning jars
   and lids, sterilized

Coarsely mash peaches in a microwave-safe 3-quart bowl, using a fork. Stir in sugar and honey. Microwave, uncovered, on high until mixture comes to a boil, about 3 minutes; stir. Microwave for an additional 8 to 11 minutes, until syrupy. Stir in lemon juice. Spoon into containers leaving 1/2-inch headspace; secure lids and freeze. Cool and refrigerate at least 8 hours before serving. Makes 2 to 3 jars.

Visit a nearby farmers' market for fresh fruits & vegetables. You may also find baked goods, jams & jellies, pickles, craft items...all kinds of unexpected treats! With indoor markets, you can visit year 'round.

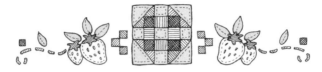

Triple Berry Jam

Linda McClain
Columbia, NJ

My son and I go berry picking in the summer and make many batches of this jam to give as holiday gifts. He loves to help pick and smash the berries.

2-1/2 c. strawberries, hulled and halved
1-1/2 c. red raspberries
1 c. black raspberries

1-3/4 oz. pkg. powdered pectin
7 c. sugar
9 1-pint canning jars and lids, sterilized

Use a potato masher to mash berries in batches. Measure 5 cups mashed fruit. Place fruit in a large stainless steel pot; add pectin. Bring to a boil, stirring constantly. Add sugar; bring to a hard boil. Boil for one minute, stirring constantly; remove from heat. Immediately spoon into hot sterilized jars, leaving 1/4-inch headspace. Wipe rims; secure with lids and rings. Process in a boiling water bath for 10 minutes; set jars on a towel to cool. Check for seals. Makes about 9 jars.

Great-grandmother had no movies, no automobiles, no airplanes, no radios...is it any wonder she wove her pleasure into patchwork quilts?

-Carrie A. Hall

A Visit to the Farmers' Market

Spicy Blueberry Jam

Robin Hill
Rochester, NY

This jam is equally good as a warmed topping on vanilla ice cream or enjoyed on breakfast muffins with a cup of coffee.

5 c. blueberries
1 T. lemon juice
1/2 t. nutmeg
3/4 c. water

1-3/4 oz. pkg. powdered pectin
5-1/2 c. sugar
5 to 6 1/2-pint canning jars
    and lids, sterilized

Thoroughly crush blueberries in a saucepan. Add lemon juice, nutmeg and water. Stir in pectin and bring to a full, rolling boil over high heat, stirring frequently. Add the sugar and return to a full rolling boil. Boil hard for one minute, stirring constantly. Remove from heat, quickly skim off foam and spoon into hot sterilized jars, leaving 1/4-inch headspace. Wipe rims; secure with lids and rings. Process in a boiling water bath for 5 minutes; set jars on a towel to cool. Check for seals. Makes 5 to 6 jars.

Wondering how much water should be in a boiling water bath? Add enough to cover canning jars by one to 2 inches. The water in the pot should remain one to 2 inches below the rim when boiling and with jars submerged.

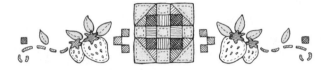

Jo Ann's Sunny Apricot Jam   *Jo Ann*

The taste of summer, captured in a jar!

3-1/2 lbs. apricots, halved and
    pitted
1/4 c. lemon juice
1-3/4 oz. pkg. powdered pectin

7 c. sugar
9 1/2-pint canning jars and
    lids, sterilized

Chop apricots finely; measure 5 cups chopped fruit into a large
saucepan. Stir in lemon juice and pectin. Bring mixture to a full rolling
boil on high heat, stirring constantly. Quickly stir in sugar. Return to
a full rolling boil and boil for one minute, stirring constantly. Remove
from heat; use a metal spoon to skim off any foam. Spoon into hot
sterilized jars, leaving 1/4-inch headspace. Wipe rims; secure with lids
and rings. Process in a boiling water bath for 10 minutes; set jars on
a towel to cool. Check for seals. Makes about 9 jars.

While Grandma's vintage canning jars with zinc lids are no
longer recommended for home canning, they can be used for
preserves that will be stored in the refrigerator. They also
make pleasing countertop storage for pasta, dried beans and
other dry goods.

Concord Grape-Plum Jelly

Shelley Turner
Boise, ID

Give this a try if your yard has an old-fashioned grape arbor or watch for Concord grapes at farmers' markets.

3 lbs. Concord grapes
3-1/2 lbs. plums, pitted
1 c. water
1-3/4 oz. pkg. powdered pectin

8-1/2 c. sugar
10 1/2-pint canning jars and
    lids, sterilized

Thoroughly crush grapes and plums in a saucepan. Add water; bring to a boil. Cover and simmer 10 minutes. Strain juice through a double layer of cheesecloth; measure 6-1/2 cups juice. Discard fruit. Combine juice with pectin in a large saucepan. Bring to a hard boil over high heat, stirring constantly. Add sugar; return to a full rolling boil. Boil hard for one minute, stirring constantly. Remove from heat and skim off foam. Quickly spoon into hot sterilized jars, leaving 1/4-inch head-space. Wipe rims; secure with lids and rings. Process in a boiling water bath for 5 minutes; set jars on a towel to cool. Check for seals. Makes about 10 jars.

Trim a big canvas tote bag with quilt squares attached with simple stitching or fabric glue. So handy for carrying home goodies from the farmers' market!

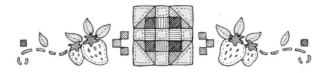

Old-Fashioned Pear Preserves

Stephanie Mayer
Portsmouth, VA

We love it on muffins and homemade bread...pancakes and waffles, too!

6 c. pears, cored, peeled and
   sliced
1 c. water
1 T. lemon juice
1-3/4 oz. pkg. powdered pectin
8 c. sugar

1/2 c. brown sugar, packed
2 t. allspice
2 t. nutmeg
6 1/2-pint canning jars and lids,
   sterilized

Combine pears, water and lemon juice in a heavy saucepan. Bring to a boil; reduce heat, cover and simmer for 10 minutes. Stir in pectin and return to a full boil. Stir in sugar; continue boiling and stirring, uncovered, for one minute, until sugar dissolves. Remove from heat; stir in brown sugar and spices. Quickly fill hot sterilized jars, leaving 1/2-inch headspace. Wipe rims; secure with lids and rings. Process in a boiling water bath for 10 minutes; set jars on a towel to cool. Check for seals. Makes 6 jars.

Share the goodness...nestle a jar of Old-Fashioned Pear Preserves and a loaf of homemade bread in a basket lined with a vintage tea towel for a welcome gift.

A Visit to the Farmers' Market

Peach-Jalapeño Jam

Sharon Demers
Dolores, CO

My husband and I love this sweet-hot jam with cream cheese and crackers. I also mix it with equal parts barbecue sauce as a glaze for grilling chicken. We like it so much, we even heat it and use as a topping over vanilla ice cream!

1 doz. peaches, peeled, halved,
    pitted and chopped
7 jalapeños, chopped
5 to 6 c. sugar

1-3/4 oz. pkg. powdered pectin
3 to 4 1-pint canning jars and
    lids, sterilized

Place peaches in a heavy saucepan; do not add water. Cook over low heat until tender but not too mushy. Add jalapeños; cook until tender. Add sugar and cook until thickened. Add pectin; cook an additional 15 minutes, stirring frequently. Spoon into hot sterilized jars, leaving 1/2-inch headspace. Wipe rims; secure with lids and rings. Process in a boiling water bath for 20 minutes; set jars on a towel to cool. Check for seals. Makes 3 to 4 jars.

Don't hesitate to ask questions at roadside stands...growers are eager to tell you how to choose the freshest, tastiest produce and how to prepare it for the best flavor.

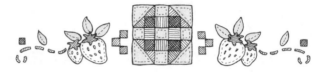

Savory Herb Bread

Lynda McCormick
Burkburnett, TX

Have a bread machine? Save time by adding everything except the olive oil to the machine and following manufacturer's instructions.

1 pkg. active dry yeast
2 t. sugar
1 c. warm water
2-1/4 c. bread flour
1/2 t. salt

1 T. fresh rosemary, chopped
1-1/2 t. fresh basil, chopped
1-1/2 t. fresh thyme, chopped
1-1/2 t. fresh oregano, chopped
1 t. olive oil

Dissolve yeast and sugar in warm water in a warmed mixer bowl. Add flour, salt and herbs. Using a dough hook, mix on low speed until well blended, about one minute. Knead on same speed for 2 additional minutes. Dough will be sticky; do not add extra flour. Place dough in a greased bowl, turning to grease top. Cover with plastic wrap, then with a heavy towel. Place in a draft-free area and let rise until double, about one hour. Turn dough out onto lightly floured wooden cutting board; rub with olive oil. Shape into a 12-inch long loaf; place on a baking stone or baking sheet. Sprinkle with topping. Bake at 350 degrees for 45 minutes or until loaf sounds hollow when tapped. Remove from pan and cool on a wire rack. Makes one loaf.

Topping:

3 T. finely shredded fresh
  Parmesan cheese

1/4 t. garlic powder
1 T. fresh rosemary, chopped

Mix ingredients together in a small bowl.

A Visit to the Farmers' Market

Fresh Herb Honey

Kathy Grashoff
Fort Wayne, IN

Tie on a sprig of fresh herbs for a delightful gift.

4 c. honey
16 sprigs fresh herbs: tarragon,
   thyme, rosemary, basil, mint,
   sage or lavender leaves

8 1/2-pint wide-mouth jars
  and lids, sterilized

Warm honey in a medium saucepan over medium heat. Lightly crush herbs; place 2 sprigs in each jar. Pour 1/2 cup warmed honey into each jar. Cover; let stand at room temperature 2 days. For gift giving, replace crushed sprigs with fresh herbs. Will keep up to 3 weeks at room temperature. Makes 8 jars.

Parsley-Chive Butter

Kim Henry
South Park, PA

Pack herb butter into ice cube trays and freeze, then pop them out, wrap and return to the freezer. When the weather turns cold, you can savor the taste of fresh-picked herbs.

1 c. butter, softened
2-1/2 T. fresh parsley, finely
   chopped

2 t. fresh chives, finely chopped
1/4 t. fresh sage, finely chopped
2 t. lemon juice

Blend together all ingredients; mix well. Makes about 1-1/4 cups.

Use uniquely shaped bottles from Grandma's pantry to display herb vinegars...they'll sparkle on a windowsill.

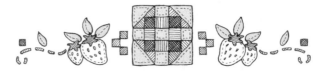

Grandma Ethel's Watermelon Pickles

Erika Wilson
Gardners, PA

So tasty that we can't imagine why we don't have them more often!

rind of 1 large watermelon
4 t. canning salt
1 qt. water
4 c. sugar
2 c. vinegar

4 t. whole cloves
8 sticks cinnamon
1/4 t. mustard
6 to 8 1-pint canning jars and
    lids, sterilized

Remove all pink flesh and green peel from watermelon rind. Cut white rind into one-inch cubes; place in a bowl. Dissolve salt in water; pour over rind and let stand overnight. (If liquid doesn't cover rind, make additional salted water with same proportions.) Drain rind and put into a saucepan; cover with plain water and simmer until almost tender. Drain again; set aside. Combine sugar and vinegar in the same saucepan; tie spices in a cheesecloth square and add to pan. Heat to boiling; remove from heat and let stand 15 minutes. Add rind to liquid and cook until transparent. Spoon rind and liquid into hot sterilized jars, leaving 1/4-inch headspace. Wipe rims; secure with lids and rings. Process in a boiling water bath for 10 minutes; set jars on a towel to cool. Check for seals. Makes 6 to 8 jars.

Planning to stop for a picnic after your morning at the farmers' market? Look for one of the new smaller watermelons...just the right size to serve 2 to 3 people.

Spiced Cucumber Rings

Hazel Kroegel
Baltimore, OH

My garden club likes to make these...they look and taste just like spiced cinnamon apple rings.

7 lbs. cucumbers, peeled, cored
   and sliced
1 c. pickling lime
1 gal. plus 2 c. water, divided
3 c. white vinegar, divided
1 T. pickling alum

1/4 c. red food coloring
10 c. sugar
8 whole cinnamon sticks
7-oz. pkg. red cinnamon candies
7 to 8 1-pint canning jars and
   lids, sterilized

Place cucumber rings in a large container. Mix lime and one gallon water; pour over cucumbers and let stand for 24 hours. Drain cucumbers; rinse in clear water 3 times. Cover with ice water and let stand 3 hours; drain. Mix one cup vinegar, alum and food coloring; pour over cucumbers. Add enough water to cover and let stand 2 hours; drain. Mix remaining vinegar, remaining water, sugar, cinnamon sticks and candies in a saucepan; bring to a boil. Pour hot mixture over cucumbers; let stand 24 hours. Drain, reserving liquid; bring liquid to a boil. Spoon cucumbers into hot sterilized jars; place one cinnamon stick in each jar. Ladle liquid over the top, leaving 1/4-inch headspace. Wipe rims; secure with lids and rings. Process in a boiling water bath for 10 minutes; set jars on a towel to cool. Check for seals. Makes 7 to 8 jars.

You'll find colorful old-fashioned cut flowers like zinnias and dwarf sunflowers at farmers' markets. Arrange a generous bunch in a Mason jar and tie with jute for a bouquet Grandma will love.

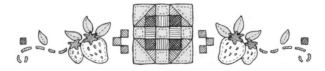

Red Pickled Beets & Eggs

Barbara Schmeckpepper
Elwood, IL

My mom made these beets and eggs every Easter...she got the recipe from my dad's mother.

3 beets, peeled and cubed
3 c. water
2 c. sugar
2 c. cider vinegar

3 T. pickling spices
1 doz. eggs, hard-boiled and peeled

Simmer beets in water in a saucepan until tender and water has turned red. Remove beets; cool and refrigerate. Reserve water in saucepan; add sugar, vinegar and pickling spices and boil for 10 minutes. Let cool; pour into a covered container and refrigerate overnight. Strain liquid; discard spices. Combine liquid, beets and eggs in a large covered container; refrigerate 2 to 3 days. Cut eggs in half just before serving. Serves 8 to 10.

Vegetables stay bright-colored and tasty if you add a tablespoon or 2 of vinegar to the water when boiling or steaming.

Red Onion Jam

Sharon Demers
Dolores, CO

This jam is great on roast beef sandwiches made with grilled sourdough bread, Havarti cheese and horseradish.

3 c. red onions, quartered and thinly sliced
1-1/2 c. apple juice
1/2 c. red wine vinegar
1-1/2 t. ground sage
1/2 t. pepper

1-3/4 oz. pkg. powdered pectin
1/2 t. butter
4 c. sugar
1/2 c. brown sugar, packed
5 to 6 1/2-pint canning jars and lids, sterilized

Put onions in a large heavy stockpot. Stir in apple juice, vinegar, sage, pepper and pectin; add butter. Bring mixture to a full rolling boil over high heat, stirring constantly. Mix sugars in a bowl; quickly stir into onion mixture. Return to a full rolling boil; boil 5 minutes, stirring constantly. Remove from heat; skim off any foam with a metal spoon. Quickly ladle into hot sterilized jars, leaving 1/8-inch headspace. Wipe rims; secure with lids and rings. Process in a boiling water bath for 5 minutes; set jars on a towel to cool. Check for seals. Makes 5 to 6 jars.

Watch for colorful snapshot opportunities at the farmers' market...picture the kids standing in a field of pumpkins or tall sunflowers!

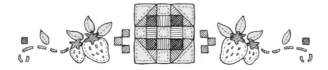

Quick Mustard Pickles

Cora Baker
La Rue, OH

These quick & easy pickles add a tangy accent to sandwiches.

16-oz. jar sweet mixed pickles,
   drained
6 T. sugar

3/4 t. ground cloves
2 T. mustard

Place pickles in a bowl. Sprinkle with sugar and cloves; mix thoroughly. Stir in mustard until pickles are coated evenly. Cover and refrigerate overnight. Makes one pint.

Remade Pickles

Emily Baker
Burgaw, NC

The taste of homemade pickles without the effort!

64-oz. jar whole kosher dill
   pickles, drained
3 c. sugar
1/2 c. vinegar

1 t. mustard seed
1 t. celery seed
17 whole cloves

Rinse pickles with cold water; slice and repack into jar. Combine sugar, vinegar, and spices; pour over pickles. Refrigerate for several days before serving. Makes 2 quarts.

Save that leftover pickle juice! It makes a tasty addition to potato salad and deviled eggs.

A Visit to the Farmers' Market

Refrigerator Pickles

Pamela Bures Raybon
Edna, TX

My mom wanted to try something different when she and Dad had a bumper crop of cucumbers. She found this recipe in a Czech heritage cookbook...everyone who tried them wanted some to take home!

16 c. cucumbers, sliced
1 onion, sliced
1 green pepper, sliced
3 c. sugar

2 c. cider vinegar
1/3 c. canning salt
1 t. celery seed
1 t. mustard seed

Combine cucumbers, onion and pepper in a gallon jar; set aside. Mix remaining ingredients in a saucepan; bring to a boil. Let cool; pour over cucumber mixture. Cover and place in refrigerator overnight. Makes one gallon.

Grandmother's beauty secret...take a little nap with a cucumber slice on each eyelid. Just 15 minutes will relax you and reduce puffy eyes.

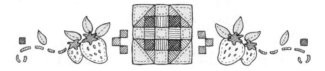

Red Tomato Relish

Sharon Crider
Lebanon, MO

You'll love the flavor of this unusual relish!

2 to 3 tomatoes, finely chopped
1 onion, finely chopped
1 green pepper, finely chopped
1/2 t. mustard seed

1/2 t. celery salt
1/2 t. salt
2 T. sugar
1/4 c. white vinegar

Combine vegetables and seasonings; mix well. Dissolve sugar in vinegar; stir into vegetables. Chill well. Makes 2 cups.

Chow-Chow

Cordelia Doss
Marshall, TX

This recipe is over 100 years old. It's good with beans, as a relish for hot dogs or all by itself.

1 head cabbage, chopped
8-oz. pkg. carrots, peeled and
    grated
1 doz. green tomatoes, chopped
8 to 10 onions, chopped
32-oz. bottle white vinegar

4 c. sugar
1 T. pickling spices, tied in
    cheesecloth
1/2 t. pickling alum
8 to 10 1-pint canning jars
    and lids, sterilized

Mix all ingredients well in a large heavy saucepan. Bring to a rolling boil; let boil for 20 minutes. Spoon into hot sterilized jars, leaving 1/4-inch headspace. Wipe rims; secure with lids and rings. Process in a boiling water bath for 10 minutes; set jars on a towel to cool. Check for seals. Makes 8 to 10 jars.

Green Tomato Relish

Kristie Rigo
Friedens, PA

A friend gave me this recipe a long time ago. We like to spread it on any sandwich, and it's especially tasty on hot dogs!

16 c. green tomatoes, finely chopped
3 green peppers, finely chopped
3 red peppers, finely chopped
3 banana peppers, finely chopped
5 onions, finely chopped
4 c. water
1 c. all-purpose flour
4 c. sugar
2-1/2 c. white vinegar
1 T. canning salt
1 t. turmeric
32-oz. jar mustard
18 1-pint canning jars and lids, sterilized

Mix tomatoes, peppers and onions; place in a colander and drain for one hour. Mix water and flour to make a paste; set aside. Mix sugar, vinegar, salt, turmeric and mustard in a large saucepan; bring to a boil. Slowly add flour mixture; cook until slightly thickened. Add tomato mixture to pan; mix well and return to a boil. Spoon into hot sterilized jars, leaving 1/4-inch headspace. Wipe rims; secure with lids and rings. Process in a boiling water bath for 10 minutes; set jars on a towel to cool. Check for seals. Makes about 18 jars.

Use a good-quality vinegar for making pickles. Either cider or white vinegar can be used...white is best for light-colored veggies such as onions and cauliflower.

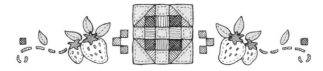

Hot Pickle Mix

Linda Behling
Cecil, PA

Fun to make in the summer when veggies are fresh in the garden...yummy in the cold days of winter! These make great gifts.

6 lbs. zucchini, cut in 1/2-inch thick slices
2 c. carrots, peeled
2 c. celery, cut in 1/2-inch thick slices
2 c. yellow peppers, cut in 1/2-inch thick slices
2 c. green peppers, cut in 1/2-inch thick slices
2 c. red peppers, cut in 1/2 inch-thick slices

2-1/2 c. pickling onions, peeled
1-1/2 c. canning salt
1 gal. plus 2 c. water, divided
10 jalapeños
3/4 c. sugar
2 T. prepared horseradish
2 cloves garlic
10 c. vinegar
10 1-pint canning jars and lids, sterilized

Combine zucchini, carrots, celery, peppers and onions in a large container. Dissolve salt in one gallon water; pour over zucchini mixture and let stand one hour. Cut 3 to 4 slits in each jalapeño; set aside. Combine remaining ingredients in a saucepan; simmer 15 minutes. Drain mixture and remove garlic; rinse and drain again thoroughly. Pack vegetables into hot sterilized jars; add one jalapeño to each jar. Ladle liquid over the top, leaving 1/4-inch headspace. Wipe rims; secure with lids and rings. Process in a boiling water bath for 10 minutes; set jars on a towel to cool. Check for seals. Makes about 10 jars.

Parsley, sage, rosemary, thyme...to enjoy the best flavor from your favorite fresh herbs, add them to recipes toward the end of the cooking period.

A Visit to the Farmers' Market

Sweet & Sour Banana Peppers

Donna Kloos
New Castle, PA

If you like hot peppers on sandwiches and pizza, you'll love these.

21 banana peppers, sliced
5 onions, sliced
2 c. white vinegar
2 c. water
1 c. sugar
2 t. salt

4 t. oil
2 t. Italian seasoning
4 cloves garlic, minced
6 1-pint canning jars and lids,
   sterilized

Combine peppers and onions in a large heavy saucepan; set aside. Combine remaining ingredients; pour over vegetables and let stand overnight. Drain and reserve liquid; bring liquid to a boil. Simmer for 15 minutes; set aside. Spoon vegetables into hot sterilized jars, leaving 1/4-inch headspace; ladle liquid over the top. Wipe rims; secure with lids and rings. Process in a boiling water bath for 10 minutes; set jars on a towel to cool. Check for seals. Makes 6 jars.

Use a damp sponge sprinkled with baking soda to scrub fruits & veggies...it works just as well as expensive cleansers for vegetables.

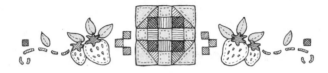

Zucchini & Onion Relish

Debi DeVore
Dover, OH

A tasty way to use up the way-too-many zucchini that are growing in your garden!

10 c. zucchini, chopped
4 c. onion, chopped
1 to 2 red peppers, chopped
4-oz. can diced green chiles
3 T. canning salt
3-1/2 c. sugar
3 c. vinegar

1 T. turmeric
4 t. celery seed
1 t. pepper
1/2 t. nutmeg
5 1-pint canning jars and lids,
   sterilized

Combine zucchini, onion, pepper, chiles and salt in a large container. Stir well and chill overnight. Rinse thoroughly; drain. Combine sugar, vinegar and spices in a large kettle; bring to a boil. Add zucchini mixture, lower heat and simmer for 10 minutes. Spoon into hot sterilized jars, leaving 1/4-inch headspace. Wipe rims; secure with lids and rings. Process in a boiling water bath for 10 minutes; set jars on a towel to cool. Check for seals. Makes 5 jars.

Grandma's flowered hankies make sentimental drawer sachets...simply fill with a scoop of dried lavender, gather up the edges and tie with a satin ribbon.

Make-a-Pickle Master Mix

Megan Brooks
Antioch, TN

In a pickle because everything looked so yummy at the farmers' market...not sure how you'll use up all the veggies you brought home? No problem! You can make tasty pickles of any firm, ripe vegetable. Add other whole herbs and spices as you like...dill, mustard seed, bay leaves, garlic, hot peppers and coriander.

8 c. vegetables, peeled and cut
    into slices, strips or flowerets
3 T. pickling spices
5 c. vinegar
2 c. water

1 c. sugar
1/4 c. canning salt
4 1-pint canning jars and lids,
    sterilized

Combine all ingredients in a large saucepan over medium heat, stirring occasionally, until sugar dissolves and mixture just begins to boil. Spoon vegetables into hot sterilized jars; pour hot liquid over vegetables. Let cool, cover and refrigerate for 2 to 3 weeks before opening. Will keep in the refrigerator for 2 months after being opened. Makes about 4 jars.

Make tangy pickled veggies next time you finish a jar of pickles! Simply cut up raw carrots, green peppers, celery and other vegetables, drop them into the leftover pickle juice and refrigerate.

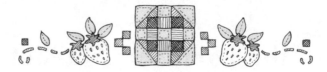

Mozzarella-Tomato Corn Muffins

Jenny Matlock
Mesa, AZ

*These are really different and yummy...they make a great light
meal with a tossed salad, and go well with white chili
or vegetable beef soup in cool weather.*

1/2 c. cornmeal
1-1/2 c. all-purpose flour
1 T. baking powder
1 t. salt
1/4 t. pepper
2 T. brown sugar, packed
2 roma tomatoes, seeded and
   diced

1/4 c. fresh basil, coarsely
   chopped
1 c. milk
1/4 c. olive oil
1 egg
8-oz. pkg. mozzarella cheese,
   cut in 3/4-inch cubes

Stir together cornmeal, flour, baking powder, salt, pepper and brown
sugar in a medium bowl. Add tomatoes and basil; toss together until
well combined and set aside. Stir together milk, oil and egg in a small
bowl; stir into dry ingredients just until blended. Divide mixture evenly
among 9 greased muffin tins. Insert one cheese cube in the center
of each muffin. Bake at 400 degrees until dark golden, about 20 to
25 minutes. Let muffins stand 5 minutes before serving. Makes 9.

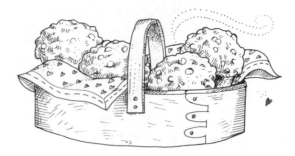

Did you buy a bunch of fresh herbs for a recipe that calls for
just a couple of tablespoons? Chop the extra herbs and add to
a tossed salad! Fresh dill, parsley, thyme, chives and basil all
add "zing" to salads.

A Visit to the Farmers' Market

Linda's Tomato Sandwiches

Stephanie Shannon
Yale, MI

Is there anything more delightful on a summer day than a simple sandwich of fresh tomatoes?

1/3 c. fat-free mayonnaise
1 t. lemon juice
1/2 t. lemon zest
1/4 t. coriander
1/4 t. salt

1/4 t. pepper
4 to 6 slices French bread,
    toasted
1 to 2 tomatoes, sliced

Blend mayonnaise, lemon juice and seasonings in a small bowl. Spread on half of bread slices; top with tomatoes and remaining bread. Makes 2 to 3 sandwiches.

Grandma knew this little trick for softening unripe fruit...simply place it in a brown paper bag on the countertop. It'll ripen in no time at all.

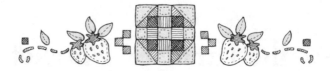

Farmers' Fried Green Tomatoes

Elizabeth Furry
Minden, NV

*My favorite farmers' market vendor gave me this recipe...a little
old man with overalls, a baseball cap and a big heart.*

1 c. all-purpose flour
2 eggs, beaten
1 c. dry Italian bread crumbs
1/2 c. shortening

2 to 3 green tomatoes, sliced
1/4-inch thick
Optional: ranch salad dressing

Place flour, eggs and bread crumbs in separate small bowls; set aside.
Heat shortening in a large skillet over medium heat. Dip each tomato
slice into the flour, then the eggs and lastly the bread crumbs. Place
tomato slices in skillet and cook until golden, about 2 minutes on each
side. Reduce heat to low and cook an additional 3 minutes or until
tender. Serve with dressing for dipping, if desired. Serves 4 to 6.

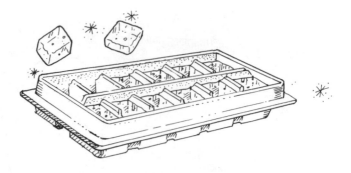

It's so easy to make flavorful vegetable broth like Grandma's.
Save up leftover veggies, even peels and scraps, in your
freezer. Cover with water and simmer gently for 30 minutes,
strain and freeze in ice cube trays. Use to make delicious
soups or add to any dish that needs a flavor boost!

A Visit to the Farmers' Market

White Bean & Tomato Salad

Denise Neal
Monument, CO

I got this delicious recipe while on vacation in England. We love it! If you can't get cannellini beans, navy beans will work fine.

15-oz. can cannellini beans, drained and rinsed
2 zucchini or yellow squash, diced
1-pt. pkg. cherry tomatoes, halved
1/2 c. red onion, chopped
3 T. olive oil
2 T. lemon juice
1/4 c. fresh cilantro, chopped

Combine all ingredients in a large bowl. Cover and refrigerate. Let stand at room temperature 20 to 30 minutes before serving. Makes 6 servings.

Write or paste favorite family recipes on 4"x6" index cards...they'll fit perfectly into a flip photo album. The album stands up easily by your stove and the plastic pages will protect your recipes.

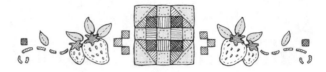

Mom's Fried Corn

Tracy Chitwood
Van Buren, MO

For us, summertime means fried corn at Mom's house!

6 ears corn, husked
1 T. bacon drippings
2 c. water

1 T. butter
salt to taste

Gently cut corn from cobs; scrape cobs with a knife to release juices and set aside. Heat drippings in a cast iron skillet over medium heat. Mix water, butter and salt with corn; add to skillet and heat, stirring often, until corn thickens and becomes tender. Serves 4 to 6.

Grilled Corn on the Cob

Paula Smith
Ottawa, IL

This is a great side dish with grilled meat!

6 ears corn, husked
1/2 c. butter, softened
1 t. salt

1/2 t. pepper
1/4 t. cayenne pepper

Place each ear of corn on a double thickness of aluminum foil. Combine butter, salt, pepper and cayenne in a small bowl; spread a heaping tablespoon over each ear of corn. Top with one ice cube on the center of each ear. Fold aluminum foil around ears; seal tightly. Grill, covered, over medium heat 25 to 30 minutes or until corn is tender, turning once. Makes 6 servings.

A little red wagon makes a whimsical planter for potted herbs...so easy to wheel to the kitchen door and snip off sprigs for cooking!

Libby's Southern Green Beans

Phyllis Peters
Three Rivers, MI

In 1950, my husband, our young children and I made a trip by car to the Southern states to visit his Army buddies. In Kentucky, we accepted an invitation to eat dinner with Libby and Edward. She fixed these delicious beans for us, picked fresh from her garden.

1/2 c. bacon drippings
2 to 2-1/2 lbs. green beans,
   cut lengthwise

salt and pepper to taste

Melt drippings in a large cast iron skillet; add beans. Simmer on low heat, covered, for 3 to 4 hours, stirring 3 to 4 times to cook evenly. During the last half hour, uncover and brown lightly. Add salt and pepper to taste. Serves 6 to 8.

Show off your favorite keepsakes in a hanging wall basket...measuring spoons, cookie cutters and recipe cards or thimbles, pincushions and pretty cards of buttons. Tuck in a small photo of Grandma and a tiny bear or rag doll from the craft store for fun.

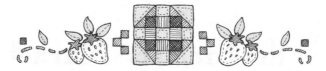

Garden Tomato Salad

Rosalie Berardo
North Brunswick, NJ

Serve with crusty Italian bread...we all think the best part is dunking your bread in the juice!

3 to 5 tomatoes, cut into
  bite-size pieces
1 cucumber, peeled and sliced
2 to 3 leaves fresh basil, finely
  chopped

2 to 3 T. red onion, chopped
1 t. garlic salt
1/2 t. dried oregano
2 T. olive oil

Mix all ingredients together. Let stand several minutes before serving. Makes 4 to 6 servings.

Cucumber Salad

Suzanne Durbano
Jacksonville, FL

Cucumbers, onions and sour cream...a classic flavor combination.

12 cucumbers, peeled and very
  thinly sliced
2 c. salt
2 onions, halved and thinly
  sliced

24-oz. container sour cream
pepper to taste

Place cucumber slices in a colander. Cover with salt and ice; let drain 8 hours, adding more ice half-way through, until cucumbers are very crisp. Combine with onions in a large bowl. Stir in sour cream; add pepper to taste. Refrigerate for several hours or overnight. Serves 14.

Laughter is brightest where food is best.

-Irish Proverb

Fresh Veggie Salad

Denise Winder
Old Fort, TN

Toss with sunflower kernels for a little extra crunch.

1 bunch broccoli, cut into
   flowerets
1 head cauliflower, cut into
   flowerets
1 doz. baby carrots, cut in thin
   strips

4-oz. can sliced black olives,
   drained
1 onion, finely chopped
16-oz. pkg. bacon, crisply
   cooked and crumbled
2 c. shredded Cheddar cheese

Combine all ingredients in a large bowl. Toss with dressing and refrigerate until serving time. Serves 10 to 12.

Dressing:

1/2 c. mayonnaise
3 T. vinegar

1/2 c. sugar

Mix ingredients well in a small bowl.

Enjoy seasonal fruits & veggies…strawberries and asparagus in spring, corn and tomatoes in summer, acorn squash and pears in fall, cabbage and apples in winter. You'll be serving your family the tastiest, healthiest produce year 'round.

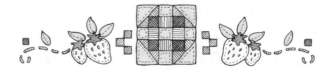

Country-Style Roast Vegetables

Mary Schlagel
Warwick, NY

*Even better made with fresh-picked herbs...just substitute
2 to 3 teaspoons fresh for one teaspoon dried herbs.*

2 potatoes, peeled and cubed
2 carrots, peeled and thickly
   sliced
1 zucchini, thickly sliced
1 yellow squash, thickly sliced
1 red pepper, cubed
2 T. olive oil

1 t. dried basil
1 t. dried parsley
1 t. dried oregano
1/2 t. salt
1/8 t. pepper
1/8 t. garlic powder
1/4 c. water

Combine all vegetables in a plastic zipping bag; set aside. Mix oil and
seasonings together; sprinkle on vegetable mixture and shake to coat.
Spoon into a 13"x9" baking pan. Sprinkle with water; cover. Bake at
375 degrees for 30 minutes; uncover during the last 10 minutes of
baking. Serves 6.

Cooking potatoes ahead for later use? Keep them light in
color by covering them with cold water and adding a
little vinegar.

A Visit to the Farmers' Market

Braised Carrots with Chervil

Kathy Stafiej
Brunswick, ME

If you can't find chervil, just add a little more parsley.

1-1/2 lbs. carrots, peeled and
  sliced
1-1/2 c. water
3-1/2 T. butter, softened and
  divided
1 T. sugar

1/2 t. salt
1/4 t. pepper
2 T. green onions, chopped
1 T. fresh parsley, chopped
1/4 t. fresh chervil, chopped

Combine carrots, water, 1-1/2 tablespoons butter, sugar, salt and pepper in a saucepan. Bring to a boil, cover and simmer until tender. Drain and toss with remaining butter, green onions and herbs. Serves 4 to 6.

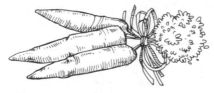

Mustard-Glazed Carrots

George Anne Thomas
Colorado Springs, CO

A surprising spicy-sweet glaze that your family will love.

2-lb. pkg. baby carrots, halved
  lengthwise
1 t. salt
3 T. butter, softened

3 T. mustard
1/4 c. brown sugar, packed
Optional: 1/4 c. fresh parsley,
  chopped

Combine carrots and salt in a medium saucepan; cover with water. Cover and simmer for 20 minutes or until tender; drain. Mix butter, mustard and brown sugar in a small saucepan. Heat for 3 minutes or until syrupy. Pour over carrots and simmer for 5 minutes. Sprinkle with parsley, if desired. Serves 6 to 8.

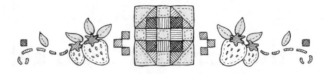

Sweet Onion Casserole

Virginia King-Hugill
Woodinville, WA

*I am happy to share my Great-Aunt Laura's recipe. She always made
sure to have this casserole waiting for us.*

1 c. margarine, softened
5 sweet onions, sliced into thin
  rings
24 round buttery crackers,
  crushed

1/2 c. grated Parmesan cheese
Optional: 2 T. milk

Melt margarine in a skillet; add onion rings and sauté over medium
heat for 15 minutes or until translucent. Spoon half of the onions into
a 1-1/2 quart baking dish. Sprinkle onions with half of the cracker
crumbs and half of the Parmesan. Repeat layering with remaining
onions, crumbs and Parmesan. Bake, uncovered, for 25 to 30 minutes
at 325 degrees. Add milk if crackers have absorbed too much liquid.
Serves 6 to 8.

Always a summer favorite...a watermelon half,
filled with melon balls, blueberries, strawberries, sliced
peaches and other fresh fruit. Toss with a little lemon juice
and honey for a tempting treat.

A Visit to the Farmers' Market

Zucchini-Corn Sauté

Mindy Aragon
Greeley, CO

We like to wrap this tasty dish in flour tortillas.

2 T. butter
1 zucchini, chopped
1 onion, chopped
1 jalapeño, diced
1/8 t. salt
1/8 t. pepper

garlic powder to taste
2 to 3 ears corn, husked and
   kernels cut off
Optional: fresh cilantro, sour
   cream

Melt butter in a skillet. Add all ingredients except corn and sauté until vegetables are tender. Stir in corn and sauté for several more minutes, until corn is tender. Garnish with fresh cilantro and sour cream, if desired. Serves 4.

Do as Grandma did...keep vinegar handy in the kitchen for all your cleaning needs. It removes stains, sanitizes and is safe on just about any surface.

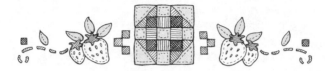

Fresh Apple Cake

Brenda Nelson
Midland, TX

This moist cake is great all by itself. It's even better with cream cheese frosting...just stir together 6 ounces cream cheese with a pound of powdered sugar.

1-1/2 c. oil
2 c. sugar
2 eggs
2-1/2 c. all-purpose flour
2 t. baking powder
1 t. baking soda

1 t. salt
2 t. vanilla extract
3 c. tart apples, cored, peeled
    and chopped
1 c. chopped pecans

Pour oil into a large mixing bowl. Add sugar and eggs; blend until creamy on low speed of hand mixer. Sift flour together with baking soda, baking powder and salt. Stir flour mixture into oil mixture, a little at a time, until well blended. Fold in apples and pecans; pour into a greased and floured 13"x9" pan. Bake at 350 degrees for 55 to 60 minutes. Serves 16.

Dress up a simple cake...lay a paper doily on top, then sprinkle with powdered sugar or baking cocoa. So dainty, yet so simple a child can do it!

A Visit to the Farmers' Market

Spicy Slow-Cooker Applesauce

Karen Tuinstra
Neshkoro, WI

Your house will smell wonderfully fragrant all day as the applesauce simmers in your slow cooker.

3 to 4 lbs. McIntosh apples,
    cored, peeled and thinly
    sliced
1/2 c. sugar
2 T. brown sugar, packed

1 t. cinnamon
1/2 t. nutmeg
1/4 c. water
2 to 3 1-pint canning jars and
    lids, sterilized

Fill slow cooker with apple slices to about 2 inches from top. Stir together sugars and spices in a small bowl; mix into apples and add water. Cover and cook on low setting for 8 hours, or until apples are tender. Mash apples with a potato masher to desired consistency. Ladle into jars, add lids and cool. Store in refrigerator. Makes 2 to 3 jars.

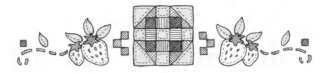

Bette's Cherry Pie

Francie Stutzman
Dalton, OH

We cannot tell a lie...this pie is scrumptious!

4 c. tart cherries, pitted and
   drained
1 c. sugar
3 T. tapioca, uncooked

1/4 t. almond extract
1 t. lemon juice
1 T. butter, melted
2 9-inch pie crusts

Combine all ingredients except crusts in a large bowl; set aside. Line a 9" pie plate with crust; pour cherry mixture over crust. Top with remaining crust; trim edges, crimp crusts together and cut slits for steam to escape. Bake at 400 degrees for 15 minutes; turn oven temperature down to 350 degrees and bake an additional 30 minutes, or until filling is thick and bubbly and crust is golden. Serves 6 to 8.

Easy Double Pie Crust

Amy Bishop
Cedar Rapids, IA

This recipe is from my 100-year-old grandmother, an Iowa farmer's wife. It's no-fail and easy for a non-cook like myself.

2 c. all-purpose flour
1/2 c. margarine

1 to 2 T. cold water
powdered sugar

Mix flour, margarine and water together just until dough rolls together. Divide in half; roll each out to a 9-inch round on wax paper that has been sprinkled with powdered sugar. Chill on wax paper before using. Makes 2 crusts.

Sky-High Strawberry Pie

Coleen Lambert
Casco, WI

Save a few perfect berries to garnish this delicious pie.

3 qts. strawberries, hulled and divided
1-1/2 c. sugar
6 T. cornstarch
2/3 c. water
Optional: several drops red food coloring

10-inch deep-dish pie crust, baked
1 c. whipping cream
1-1/2 T. instant vanilla pudding mix

In a large bowl, mash berries to equal 3 cups; set aside along with remaining whole berries. Combine sugar and cornstarch in a large saucepan. Stir in mashed berries and water; mix well. Bring to a boil over medium heat, stirring constantly; heat and stir for 2 minutes. Remove from heat; add food coloring if desired. Pour mixture into a large bowl; chill for 20 minutes, stirring occasionally, until mixture is just slightly warm. Fold in remaining whole berries. Pour into prepared pie crust; chill for 2 to 3 hours. Place cream in a small mixing bowl; use a hand mixer to whip cream and pudding mix until soft peaks form. Spread whipped cream mixture around edge of pie or dollop on individual slices. Serves 8 to 10.

Why save pie just for dessert? Invite family & friends for a pie social...everyone brings their favorite pie, and you provide the ice cream and whipped topping.

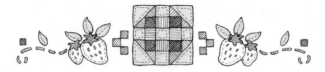

Peaches & Cookies Dessert

Amber Beagley
Nampa, ID

Substitute raspberries and raspberry-flavored gelatin for an equally tasty variation.

16-oz. pkg. shortbread cookies, divided
14-oz. can sweetened condensed milk
1/4 c. lemon juice
8-oz. container frozen whipped topping, thawed

3-oz. pkg. peach gelatin mix
1 T. cornstarch
1 c. sugar
2 c. water
1/8 t. salt
4 to 5 c. peaches, peeled, halved, pitted and sliced

Arrange whole cookies in the bottom of a 13"x9" baking pan, reserving several cookies; set aside. Mix together condensed milk and lemon juice in a bowl. Stir in whipped topping and spoon over cookies; set aside. In a saucepan, mix gelatin, cornstarch, sugar, water and salt; boil together until clear. Let cool; stir in peaches. Spoon over creamy layer; crush reserved cookies and sprinkle over top. Refrigerate until firm. Makes 8 to 10 servings.

Take the kids to a nearby pick-your-own peach orchard or strawberry farm...give them each a bucket and pretend not to notice when they nibble on their pickings!

Blueberry-Marshmallow Delight

Diane Schenck
Tumwater, WA

My mom got this recipe over 40 years ago from the owner of a local blueberry field. It's a family favorite that is expected at our family picnic every year.

2 c. graham cracker crumbs
1/3 c. sugar
1/2 c. butter, melted
28 to 30 marshmallows

1/2 c. milk
2 c. whipping cream, whipped
2 to 3 c. blueberries

Mix together cracker crumbs, sugar and butter; press half of mixture into a 13"x9" baking pan. Bake at 350 degrees for 10 minutes; let cool. Combine marshmallows and milk in the top of a double boiler. Heat over boiling water, stirring occasionally, until marshmallows are melted; cool. Combine whipped cream and blueberries; fold into marshmallow mixture. Spread over baked crumbs in pan. Sprinkle remaining crumbs over top; refrigerate several hours. Serves 8 to 10.

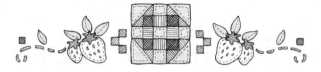

Irene's Blackberry Dumplings

Zona Hill
New Albany, IN

When my children were young, we lived in a house behind my mom & dad's. In 1966 my mom amazed us by walking through 19 inches of snow to bring us freshly baked blackberry dumplings. The memory of her doing that for us will live in my heart forever.

1 qt. blackberries
1 c. plus 1 T. sugar, divided
3/4 t. salt, divided
1/2 t. lemon extract
1-1/2 c. all-purpose flour

2 t. baking powder
1/4 t. nutmeg
2/3 c. milk
Garnish: frozen whipped
  topping, thawed

Combine blackberries, one cup sugar, 1/4 teaspoon salt and lemon extract in a Dutch oven. Bring to a boil; reduce heat and simmer for 5 minutes. In a mixing bowl, combine flour, baking powder, nutmeg, remaining sugar and remaining salt. Add milk; stir just until mixed to form a thick dough. Drop by tablespoonfuls onto hot blackberry mixture. Cover Dutch oven tightly and simmer for 15 minutes or until a toothpick inserted in a dumpling comes out clean. Garnish with whipped topping. Makes 6 to 8 servings.

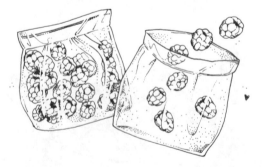

It's easy to store fresh berries to enjoy later.
Simply place berries in a single layer on a baking sheet and freeze, then store in plastic freezer bags. Frozen this way, it's convenient to remove just the amount of berries you need for a recipe.

Old-Fashioned Rhubarb Sauce

Jen Sell
Farmington, MN

*This sauce brings back the sweetest memories of my childhood.
My neighbor's mom always used to make this...it's yummy served
by itself and it's good on vanilla ice cream too.*

4 c. rhubarb, chopped   1/2 c. water
3/4 c. sugar

Combine all ingredients in a saucepan; bring to a boil, stirring
occasionally. Reduce heat to low; simmer for 10 to 12 minutes or until
rhubarb is tender. Continue to stir until rhubarb breaks up and thickens
slightly. Serves 4 to 6.

Pick up a fruit crate or 2 at the farmers' market...they make
handy carriers for cookout supplies.

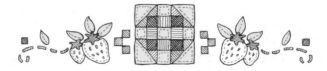

Glorious Grapes

Joan White
Malvern, PA

The cheesecake-like topping is good with all sorts of fresh fruit.

8-oz. pkg. cream cheese,
  softened
1/2 c. sugar
1 c. sour cream

1/2 t. vanilla extract
2 to 2-1/2 lbs. seedless green
  grapes

Use a hand mixer to blend cream cheese and sugar in a large bowl until well blended. Add sour cream and vanilla; mix thoroughly. Stir in the grapes. Refrigerate 8 hours or overnight. Serves 6 to 8.

Use Grandma's teacups for the prettiest flower arrangement...just group several cups together and float a single large blossom in each.

A Visit to the Farmers' Market

Chilled Cantaloupe Soup

Jacqueline Kurtz
Reading, PA

A refreshing change of pace for warm-weather days!

1 cantaloupe, peeled, seeded and
   cubed
2 c. orange juice, divided

1 T. lime juice
1/4 to 1/2 t. cinnamon
Optional: fresh mint

Combine cantaloupe and 1/2 cup orange juice in a blender or food processor. Cover and process until smooth. Transfer to a large bowl; stir in lime juice, cinnamon and remaining orange juice. Cover and chill for at least one hour. Garnish with mint, if desired. Makes about 6 servings.

Look for heirloom fruits & vegetables at the farmers' market...old-timers that Grandma knew and loved. With amusing names like Country Gentleman corn, Arkansas Traveler tomatoes, Calico Crowder peas and Jenny Lind melons, they offer a delicious taste of the good old days.

Scrapbooking

Remember how much fun you used to have playing with paper and scissors? Pick up a few fun supplies at your local craft store...a variety of colored and patterned papers, decorative-edged scissors, stickers and glue. Get out your box of family photos and spend an afternoon creating. You'll be scrapbooking in no time at all!

"Acid-free" is the magic word to look for on scrapbooking supplies...it ensures that your memory projects will last a long time.

Make your scrapbook easy to read...title each page with a family member's name or a subject using fun markers or simply stick-on letters. "Skyler," "Elizabeth," "Our Summer at the Beach," "The Wilson Family Reunion" all catch the reader's eye right away.

Scrapbooking

Color photocopies of family quilts, samplers and doilies make special background pages for scrapbooking.

Make color photocopies of black & white or sepia-toned photographs for scrapbooking, rather than black & white copies. You'll capture the old-fashioned look and feel of the photos. Use your own handwriting to label photos and add details in your scrapbook...it adds a personal touch that a computer font can't match.

Grandma's favorite

greetings from
TENNESSEE

Save all kinds of small items for scrapbooking...letters, programs, clippings, menus, award certificates and postcards. Snippets like these will really personalize your scrapbook.

Copy, color and cut these fun labels to share homemade jellies and pickles with family & friends!

from the kitchen of:

Grandma's Jam

Copy Grandma's photo onto this label.

Write a personal message on this sweet jar topper.

Hail, Hail, the Gang's all Here

Potluck & buffet favorites

Dad's Barbecue for a Crowd

Loree Matson
Fort Wayne, IN

*My dad came up with this recipe from scratch. It makes
quite a lot...freeze some and enjoy it later!*

8-1/2 lb. boneless pork roast
6-lb. boneless beef rump roast
4 onions, finely diced
3 T. plus 1 t. Worcestershire
   sauce
5-1/3 c. catsup
2 qts. plus 3/4 c. water

3-1/3 c. thick & spicy barbecue
   sauce
1 T. salt
1 t. pepper
1/4 c. white vinegar
4 doz. hamburger buns

Place roasts in 2 large stockpots; cover with water. Bring each to a boil
over high heat; reduce heat and simmer until very tender, about 3 to
4 hours. Let cool. Shred roasts; measure 10 packed cups pork and
9 packed cups beef. Combine onions, Worcestershire sauce, catsup,
water, barbecue sauce, salt and pepper in a saucepan. Heat until
boiling; add meats and vinegar. Simmer until mixture reaches desired
thickness. Spoon onto buns. Makes about 4 dozen sandwiches.

Start small for your first family reunion...invite just
your immediate family, grandparents, brothers & sisters
and their children to a simple picnic or barbecue.
You'll have a great time!

Hail, Hail, the Gang's all Here

Salisbury Steak

Cindy Watson
Gooseberry Patch

Mom used to make this for all the young men that helped Dad work the hay fields on our dairy farm. Dad never had trouble finding helpers as word spread quickly of Mom's great cooking!

1-1/2 lb. ground beef
3/4 c. instant oats, uncooked
1/4 c. onion, chopped
1 t. salt

1/4 t. pepper
1 egg
1/2 c. tomato juice
2 to 4 t. all-purpose flour

Combine all ingredients except flour; mix well. Shape into 6 steaks and brown in a skillet, reserving drippings. Arrange steaks in a 9"x9" baking dish; set aside. Add flour to drippings in skillet; cook and stir until thickened, to make gravy. Pour gravy over steaks. Bake at 350 degrees for 45 minutes to one hour. Serves 6.

Start planning your reunion early...3 months isn't too far in advance! Everyone will find it easier to reserve the date and you'll be a more relaxed hostess.

Fried Catfish

Debbie Nemecek
Springfield, IL

My dad fishes all summer and brings home freezer bags full of fish fillets. Everyone loves it prepared this way and they beg for more!

3 lbs. catfish fillets
12-oz. can beer
2 T. baking soda
2 c. milk
1 egg

1 T. salt
1 T. pepper
Optional: 2 T. Cajun seasoning
16-oz. pkg. fish breading mix
oil for frying

Soak fish in beer and baking soda for one hour. Combine milk, egg, salt, pepper and Cajun seasoning, if using. Drain fish and dip into milk mixture, then roll in breading. Heat oil in a skillet; fry fish a few at a time until golden. Serves 5.

Hushpuppies

Sandy Fine
Columbia, MO

These hushpuppies are really good at a fish fry, especially with catfish! I make them just before the fish are done. A crowd pleaser...good with butter or honey.

2 c. yellow cornmeal
1 c. all-purpose flour
1/4 c. sugar
1 T. baking powder
1 T. onion, minced

1 egg
14-3/4 oz. can cream-style corn
salt and pepper to taste
oil for deep frying

Mix all ingredients in a large bowl. Drop by tablespoonfuls into hot oil in a deep fryer; fry until golden. Makes about 3 dozen.

Janet Sue's Crab Cakes

Janet Sue Burns
Granbury, TX

This is a great recipe to fix ahead of time and freeze.

3 lbs. crabmeat
1-1/4 c. mayonnaise
3 eggs
1/4 c. onion, minced
3/4 t. seasoned salt
1/8 t. pepper

2 T. dry mustard
3/4 c. pimentos, diced
1 c. green pepper, diced
1 T. Worcestershire sauce
1-1/4 c. dry bread crumbs

Separate and flake the crabmeat with a fork; set aside. Combine mayonnaise, eggs, onion, seasonings, pimentos, peppers and Worcestershire sauce in a bowl. Add crabmeat; mix well. Fold in bread crumbs; divide into 16 portions and shape into patties. Arrange on a baking sheet and bake at 425 degrees for 10 to 15 minutes until golden. Makes 16.

Copies of cherished family photos can be made quickly and inexpensively at your local camera store or drugstore...attach them to the front of plain cards for family reunion invitations that will get everyone in the spirit!

Johnny Marzetti

Heather Neibar
South Bend, IN

This hearty dish brings back childhood memories of both family potlucks and school cafeteria meals.

1 to 1-1/2 lbs. ground beef
1-1/2 oz. pkg. Sloppy Joe mix
6-oz. can tomato paste
1-1/4 c. water
4 c. prepared elbow macaroni

15-oz. can corn, drained
8-oz. pkg. shredded Cheddar
   cheese, divided
Optional: 4-oz. can sliced
   mushrooms, drained

Brown ground beef in a skillet; drain. Stir in seasoning mix, tomato paste and water; heat and stir briefly until blended. Spoon into a 13"x9" baking dish; stir in macaroni, corn, one cup cheese and mushrooms, if desired. Bake, uncovered, at 350 degrees for 45 minutes. Sprinkle with remaining cheese; return to oven until cheese melts. Serves 4 to 6.

Have reunion guests each bring a baby photo. Have a contest...the first person to guess who's who gets a prize!

Hail, Hail, the Gang's all Here

Tuna Noodle Casserole

Lisa Bowman
Mooresville, IN

A family favorite...yummy and filling!

16-oz. pkg. wide egg noodles,
   cooked
2 10-3/4 oz. cans cream of
   mushroom soup
1 to 2 6-oz. cans tuna, drained
1 c. frozen peas, thawed

4-oz. can sliced mushrooms,
   drained
1 to 2 c. milk
salt and pepper to taste
8-oz. pkg. shredded Cheddar
   cheese

Combine noodles, soup, tuna, peas and mushrooms; stir in enough milk to moisten well. Add salt and pepper to taste. Spread in a 13"x9" baking dish; sprinkle with cheese. Bake at 350 degrees for 25 minutes. Serves 6.

Don't forget nametags at your family reunion! Use a different color of tag for each family...make it easy to see which branch of the family tree each person comes from.

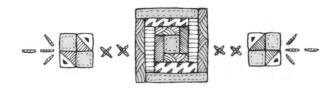

Grandma Nemeth's Chowder

Stephanie Erikson
Tustin, MI

Grandma Nemeth put her heart into everything she cooked.
I'll always remember her making this chowder.

1 onion, diced	3 potatoes, diced
1 T. butter	2 c. corn
2 T. all-purpose flour	4 slices bacon, crisply cooked
4 c. chicken broth	and crumbled
2 c. milk	salt and pepper to taste

Sauté onion in butter in a stockpot; sprinkle flour into pot and heat for 3 minutes. Add broth, milk, potatoes, corn and bacon; simmer about 45 minutes until potatoes are soft. Add salt and pepper to taste. Makes 4 to 6 servings.

Tuck sweet family photos on wire picks into
a floral centerpiece...a great conversation starter for
reunion guests.

Sauerkraut Soup

Margaret Peterson
Forest City, IA

My brother, sister and I live together. We lived on a farm for many years, and I also worked for 25 years at a drive-in restaurant. I like to try new recipes, especially those with unusual ingredients like this soup. Oh yes...I'm 84, my brother is 87 and my sister is 91.

1 to 2 lbs. Kielbasa, coarsely
   chopped
1 onion, chopped
1/2 c. all-purpose flour
1-1/4 t. dried thyme
1 t. pepper

6 c. milk
2 c. half-and-half
15-oz. can sauerkraut
1/4 c. fresh parsley, finely
   chopped

Put sausage and onion into a stockpot. Sauté over medium heat until lightly browned, about 8 minutes. Combine flour, thyme and pepper; add to sausage and heat until mixture bubbles. Stir in milk and half-and-half; continue cooking until bubbling resumes. Add sauerkraut and juice; bring to a boil. Reduce heat and continue cooking to desired thickness. Sprinkle with parsley. Serves 6 to 8.

Create a family cookbook! Have everyone share their favorite recipes and any memories or even photos that go with the recipes. The copy shop can easily make copies and bind them...everyone will want one!

Company Beef Brisket

Diana Smith
Saint Louis, MO

This recipe has been in my family for years. It is an old standby for entertaining...always turns out perfectly. It is an elegant roast, easy to prepare, slice and serve.

4-lb. boneless beef brisket	1 clove garlic, minced
2 t. salt	3 onions, thickly sliced
1/2 t. pepper	1 c. hot water

Place brisket, fat-side up, on a rack in a 13"x10" roasting pan. Sprinkle with salt, pepper and garlic. Place sliced onions on top of brisket to cover entire surface of meat. Bake at 350 degrees for one hour or until onions turn golden. Add water to pan; cover with aluminum foil, sealing tightly. Reduce heat to 300 degrees; bake for 2 additional hours. Remove roast to a platter; slice and serve with gravy. Makes 12 to 16 servings.

Gravy:

pan juices from roast	1 c. cold water
2 T. cornstarch	

Place roasting pan with pan juices on a stove burner over medium heat. Dissolve cornstarch in water; add to juices in pan, cook and stir until boiling and thickened.

Make sure your reunion is kid-friendly! With lots of games, craft supplies, music players and snacks available, your family's next generation will be so excited to come to future reunions.

Hail, Hail, the Gang's all Here

Creamy Baked Chicken

Carol Skowronnek
Streamwood, IL

This delicious dish is great for company. It goes very well with rice or noodles and steamed green veggies.

8 boneless, skinless chicken breasts
2 2-1/2 oz. pkgs. dried beef slices
10-3/4 oz. can cream of mushroom soup
1/2 c. cooking sherry or milk
1 c. grated Parmesan cheese

Wrap chicken in beef slices; arrange in a greased 13"x9" baking pan. Mix soup, sherry or milk and cheese; pour over chicken. Bake at 350 degrees for 35 to 45 minutes until tender. Makes 8 servings.

Oven Barbecued Chicken

Fran Sanchez
San Antonio, TX

A surprising and tasty way to make barbecued chicken, with a secret ingredient...barbecue potato chips!

3 to 4 lbs. boneless, skinless chicken breasts, cubed
1/2 c. margarine, melted
5-1/2 oz. bag barbecue potato chips, crushed
garlic powder to taste

Dip chicken in margarine; roll in chips and sprinkle with garlic powder. Arrange on a baking pan that has been lightly sprayed with non-stick vegetable spray. Bake at 350 degrees for one hour. Serves 4 to 6.

Need an extra-big cooler for soft drinks at the reunion? Just fill a child's plastic pool with ice!

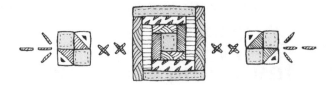

Redskin Potato Salad

Jeanne Hodack
Norwich, NY

You can't have a potluck without potato salad!

6 to 8 redskin potatoes, boiled
    and cubed
2 t. Dijon mustard
2 t. white wine vinegar

1 t. dried oregano
2 T. oil
4 to 6 green onions, sliced
salt and pepper to taste

Place potatoes in a serving bowl; set aside. Whisk together remaining ingredients; pour over potatoes. Toss well. Chill before serving. Serves 8 to 10.

Nostalgia is like a grammar lesson: you find the present tense,
but the past perfect!

-Owens Lee Pomeroy

Sweet Potato Pone

Nelle Stinson-Smith
Mobile, AL

An old-fashioned dish that can double as either a side or a dessert.

6 c. sweet potatoes, grated
1 T. vanilla extract
1 T. cinnamon
1 t. ground cloves
1 t. allspice
1/8 t. nutmeg

1/8 t. salt
1/2 c. butter, softened
1-1/2 c. sugar
4 eggs, beaten
6 T. maple-flavored syrup
1 to 1-1/2 c. milk

Mix all ingredients together with enough milk to make soupy; pour into a 13"x9" baking pan. Bake at 325 degrees for one hour; cool. Cut into squares. Serves 12 to 15.

Your neighborhood copy shop can easily create family photo calendars for you. Just choose a dozen heartfelt family photos...snow fun for January, kids at the swimming pool for July and trick-or-treaters for October.

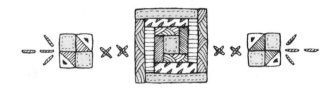

Hometown Corn Bake

Susie Backus
Gooseberry Patch

This dish was always served at family potlucks and Thanksgiving dinners in my hometown in Iowa. I still make it now that I live in Ohio...it reminds me of home.

15-oz. can corn
15-oz. can cream-style corn
1/2 c. butter, melted

1 c. sour cream
2 eggs, beaten
7-oz. pkg. cornbread mix

Mix all ingredients together; spoon into a 13"x9" baking pan. Bake at 350 degrees for one hour or until golden. Serves 8.

Capture family members' memories on videotape. Let the kids be junior reporters and think of questions to ask...what was your typical school day like? who was the most famous person you ever met? do you remember the first time you rode on a Ferris wheel? You'll all treasure these precious recollections.

Sweet Baked Beans

Elisabeth Lynch
Schiller Park, IL

This easy, tasty recipe is always a treat at picnics.

1 onion, chopped
5 cloves garlic, minced
1 T. oil
1/2 c. brown sugar, packed
1/2 c. white vinegar
2 t. dry mustard
1/2 c. molasses

15-1/2 oz. can kidney beans,
   drained and liquid reserved
15-1/2 oz. can lima beans
15-1/2 oz. butter beans
16-oz. can baked beans
8 slices bacon, crisply cooked
   and crumbled

Sauté onion and garlic in oil in a saucepan. Add brown sugar, vinegar, mustard and molasses; simmer 3 to 5 minutes. Combine all the beans in a 2-quart baking dish. Pour mixture over beans; add bacon. If beans look too thick, add some of reserved kidney bean liquid. Cover and bake at 350 degrees for 45 minutes; uncover and bake an additional 5 minutes. Makes 6 to 8 servings.

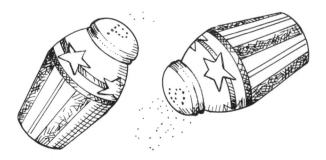

Picknicking outside on a hot, humid day? Keep salt free-flowing by placing a few dry grains of rice in the shaker.

Spinach Salad & Hot Bacon Dressing

Kristie Rigo
Friedens, PA

Your guests will love the tasty combination of flavors in this salad.

10-oz. bag spinach, torn into
    bite-size pieces
4 eggs, hardboiled, peeled and
    sliced

1 tomato, chopped
1 red onion, sliced
8 to 10 mushrooms, sliced

Toss all ingredients together; serve with hot dressing. Serves 4.

Dressing:

1/2 to 1 lb. bacon, cut into
    one-inch pieces
1 onion, chopped
1 clove garlic, minced
1/2 c. brown sugar, packed

1/2 c. red wine vinegar
2 c. water, divided
salt and pepper to taste
1 T. cornstarch

Sauté together bacon, onion and garlic until bacon is crisp. Add brown sugar, vinegar, 1-1/2 cups water, salt and pepper; simmer until mixture cooks down by half. Mix together cornstarch and remaining water; add to pan and simmer until thick and bubbly.

Ask everyone to bring a family keepsake for sharing at the reunion...Grandmother's favorite songbook, Aunt Mary's sunbonnet, Cousin John's ukelele. Be sure to make time for telling the stories behind these treasures.

Reuben Toss Salad

Sally Bourdlaies
Bay City, MI

This salad was always a big hit at our son's scouting banquets. When I'm short on time, I pick up ingredients from the grocery store's salad bar and add bottled Thousand Island salad dressing.

27-oz. pkg. sauerkraut, drained
  and rinsed
1 c. carrots, peeled and grated
1 c. green pepper, chopped
8-oz. pkg. sliced Swiss cheese,
  cut in thin strips

8-oz. pkg. deli corned beef,
  thinly sliced and cut in thin
  strips
2 slices rye bread, toasted,
  buttered and cubed

Mix all ingredients together; toss with dressing. Serves 6 to 8.

Dressing:

1/2 c. mayonnaise
2 T. chili sauce

1 T. milk
onion to taste, chopped

Combine all ingredients; mix well.

Set up old-timey games like badminton and croquet for a reunion icebreaker that will bring all ages together! Indoors, try favorite board games or even a big jigsaw puzzle.

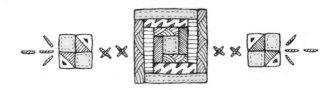

Great-Grandma's Nut Bread

Lora Montgomery
Gooseberry Patch

I remember having this nut bread at Christmas from the time I was a little girl. My mom would make it to give to teachers, the mailman, the bus driver, because you could make it ahead and it traveled well.

2 eggs, beaten
1-1/4 c. sugar
1-1/2 c. milk
1 T. butter, melted

1 c. walnuts or pecans, chopped
3 c. all-purpose flour
4 t. baking powder
1/2 t. salt

Mix eggs, sugar, milk, butter and nuts together; set aside. Combine flour, baking powder and salt; stir into egg mixture. Pour into 2 greased 9"x5" loaf pans; let stand 40 minutes. Bake at 325 degrees for 40 minutes to one hour. Makes 16 servings.

Invite the musicians in the family to entertain at your reunion! Whether it's bluegrass fiddle, classical piano or the guitar, your family is sure to enjoy listening and singing along.

Mashed Potato Bread

Camille Guy
Chillicothe, OH

I've made this delicious bread for 30 years...my family can't get enough of it! I've won blue ribbons at our county fair with this recipe.

1 pkg. active dry yeast
1/2 c. warm water
1 c. milk
2/3 c. shortening
1/2 c. sugar

1 c. mashed potatoes, warmed
1 T. salt
2 eggs, beaten
6 c. all-purpose flour

Dissolve yeast in water in a small bowl; set aside. Heat milk to just below boiling point; add shortening, sugar, potatoes and salt and allow to cool. Add dissolved yeast and eggs; mix well. Add enough flour to make a soft dough just stiff enough to handle. Place dough on lightly floured board and knead until smooth and satiny, about 8 minutes. Allow to rise until double. Divide dough in half; shape and place in 2 greased 9"x5" loaf pans. Allow to rise again; bake at 350 degrees for 30 minutes. Makes 16 servings.

No cowboy was ever faster on the draw than a grandparent pulling a baby picture out of a wallet.

-Unknown

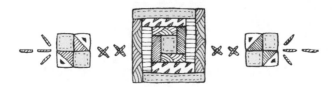

Slow-Cooker Sloppy Joes

Shelley Sparks
Amarillo, TX

*It's great to start this in the morning and have it waiting for you
when everyone arrives home hungry at dinnertime.*

1-1/2 lbs. ground beef
1 c. onion, chopped
2 cloves garlic, minced
3/4 c. catsup
1/2 c. green pepper, chopped
1/2 c. celery, chopped
1/4 c. water

1 T. brown sugar, packed
2 T. mustard
2 T. vinegar
2 T. Worcestershire sauce
1-1/2 t. chili powder
6 to 8 hamburger buns, toasted

In a skillet, brown beef, onion and garlic; drain and set aside. Combine
remaining ingredients except buns in a slow cooker; stir in beef
mixture. Cover; cook on low setting for 6 to 8 hours or on high setting
for 3 to 4 hours. Spoon onto buns. Serves 6 to 8.

Slow cookers are perfect potluck helpers! Just plug them in
and they'll do the work for you.

Barbecued Beef Sandwiches

JoEllen Ferington
Fountain Hills, AZ

Add coleslaw and potato chips and you have a complete meal!

1/2 c. celery, minced	2 T. lemon juice
1 onion, minced	1-1/2 t. mustard
1-1/2 c. catsup	3/4 c. water
3 T. Worcestershire sauce	1 t. salt
3 T. brown sugar, packed	3 to 3-1/2 lb. beef chuck roast
2 T. cider vinegar	6 to 8 hamburger buns

Combine all ingredients except roast and buns in a medium saucepan. Simmer for 5 minutes, stirring occasionally. Cut roast in 2 to 3 pieces; place in a single layer in a roasting pan. Pour sauce mixture over roast. Cover and bake at 350 degrees for 2 to 3 hours, turning roast about every 30 minutes. Remove cover for last 30 minutes; sauce will thicken. Shred meat; discard excess fat and any bone. Serve on buns. Serves 6 to 8.

Make photo transfers of Grandma & Grandpa's wedding picture. Iron onto a ready-made canvas tote bags and outline with tea-dyed lace...a heartfelt souvenir for an anniversary celebration.

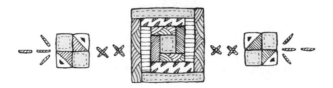

Callie Coe's Chicken & Dumplings

Marilyn Meyers
Orange City, FL

My grandma always made her chicken & dumplings for family reunions. She would roll out the dough with a jelly glass.

3 to 4 lbs. chicken
3 qts. water
salt and pepper to taste

4 eggs, hard-boiled, peeled
and chopped

Place chicken pieces in a large pot; add water. Bring to a boil; reduce heat and simmer until tender and juices run clear, about an hour. Remove chicken, reserving broth in pot. Let chicken cool; remove bones and return meat to chicken broth. Add chopped eggs. Bring broth to a boil and add dumplings one at a time; stir well before adding each new batch of dumplings. After adding last batch, put lid on the pot and simmer until tender, about 20 minutes. Remove from heat; let stand a few minutes before serving. Serves 4 to 6.

Dumplings:

4 c. self-rising flour

1 to 1-1/4 c. warm water

Mix flour with enough water to make a dough that can be rolled out. Divide dough into 4 batches. Roll out each batch of dough 1/2-inch thick on a lightly floured surface; cut into strips.

Post a big family tree at your gathering...have everyone bring a small photo of themselves and attach to the right branch. A great way for everyone to see where they fit into the family!

Homestyle Chicken Pot Pie

Lorri Young
Poolesville, MD

A real made-from-scratch pot pie, hearty and satisfying.

6 potatoes, cut into bite-size
  pieces
2 carrots, peeled and chopped
3/4 c. butter
2 stalks celery, chopped
1 c. onion, chopped
1 c. frozen peas

2 T. all-purpose flour
1-1/2 c. chicken broth
1 c. half-and-half
4 boneless, skinless chicken
  breasts, cooked and
  shredded
9-inch pie crust

Sauté potatoes and carrots in butter; add celery, onion and peas. Cook for 5 minutes or until peas are thawed; stir in flour to coat vegetables. Pour in broth; stir until mixture thickens. Add half-and-half; stir until sauce is thick and creamy. Mix in chicken; pour into a greased 2-quart baking dish. Cover with pie crust; shape edges of crust and cut slits in top. Bake at 350 degrees for 30 minutes or until golden. Makes 4 servings.

Picnicking at the family homestead? Some flowers will continue to thrive and bloom decades after the original homeowners have moved on. Share cuttings, seeds or divisions to take home and plant...how delightful to know that the peonies, hollihocks or roses you treasure were first enjoyed by Grandma.

Savory Parmesan Slices

Jackie Sampson
Central City, NE

*Why buy prepackaged garlic bread when it's so easy
to make it yourself?*

1 loaf French bread, sliced
1/2 c. butter, softened
1/8 t. garlic salt
1 c. mayonnaise

1/2 c. grated Parmesan cheese
1/2 c. onion, chopped
1/8 t. Worcestershire sauce
1/8 t. hot pepper sauce

Spread bread slices with butter; arrange on an ungreased baking sheet.
Sprinkle with garlic salt; set aside. Combine remaining ingredients and
spread on bread. Bake at 350 degrees for 15 minutes. Serves 8 to 10.

Just before everyone "digs in," take a snapshot of
Grandma's special pie or the casserole that everyone
always begs Aunt Betty to bring! Frame it with the actual
recipe for a family memento.

Easy Dinner Rolls

Michele Cutler
Sandy, UT

I've been making these light, tasty rolls ever since I was first married in 1969. My oldest daughter requests them at every family occasion.

2 T. active dry yeast
1/2 c. sugar
2 c. warm water
2 eggs, beaten

1/2 c. oil
1 T. salt
4 to 5 c. all-purpose flour
Garnish: butter

Dissolve yeast and sugar in water; let stand for 5 minutes. Add eggs, oil and salt; mix well. Stir in flour until dough is very sticky; do not knead. Allow dough to rise 1-1/2 hours. Using as little additional flour as possible, form 2-inch balls and arrange them on a lightly greased baking sheet. Let rise 45 minutes; bake at 400 degrees for 12 minutes. Brush tops with butter and serve warm. Makes about 2-1/2 dozen.

Make family stepping stones! Line a pizza box with plastic and pour in ready-mix cement...just follow the package directions. Let the kids press in their hands or feet and inscribe their names. It'll be such fun at the next reunion to see how they've grown!

Zucchini Fritters

Julie Milliken
Lakewood, CO

You'll definitely want a big platter of tasty munchies for chatting and getting reacquainted at your reunion.

1 c. zucchini, grated
1 c. carrots, peeled and grated
2 T. onion, chopped
1/2 to 3/4 c. all-purpose flour

1/4 t. salt
1/4 t. pepper
1/8 t. seasoning salt
1/4 to 1/2 c. oil

Mix together all ingredients except oil; set aside. Heat oil in a skillet; drop vegetable mixture into skillet by tablespoonfuls. Sauté until golden and vegetables are tender. Serve warm. Makes about 2 dozen.

Jo Ann's Sausage-Stuffed Mushrooms

Jo Ann

Bet you can't eat just one!

6 oz. ground sweet Italian
    sausage
1 clove garlic, minced
3 T. olive oil

2 T. fresh parsley, minced
1/4 c. grated Parmesan cheese
16 mushrooms, stems removed

Brown sausage and garlic in oil; drain. Stir in parsley and Parmesan cheese. Spoon mixture into mushrooms. Arrange in a 13"x9" baking dish; bake at 350 degrees for 20 minutes. Serve warm. Makes 16.

State Fair Hot Sausage Balls

Mary Henson
Eaton, OH

Substitute a mild-flavored sausage if you prefer.

1 lb. ground hot sausage
2 c. biscuit baking mix

10-oz. pkg. shredded sharp
Cheddar cheese

Mix all ingredients together; shape into one-inch balls. Arrange in a 13"x9" baking pan; bake at 375 degrees for 18 minutes. Serve warm. Makes 1-1/2 to 2 dozen.

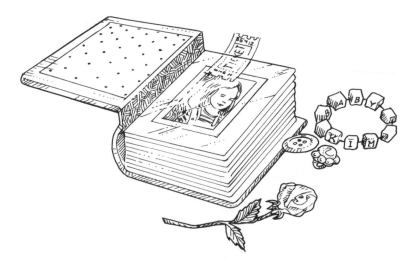

No time to make a full-size scrapbook? Try a small flip photo album...attach small mementos like ticket stubs, pressed flowers, buttons and tiny seashells to index cards for some pages, and fill the rest with snapshots from your event. Your little book will quickly fill up with memories!

Monkey Bread

Mary Schmidt
Freeport, IL

*Kids love to pull apart this spicy, caramel-y treat...adults think
it's yummy too!*

1/2 c. butter
1 c. brown sugar, packed
3 T. cinnamon, divided

1/2 c. sugar
2 12-oz. tubes refrigerated
   biscuits, cut in quarters

Melt butter, brown sugar and one tablespoon cinnamon in a small
saucepan. Heat until bubbly; set aside. Blend sugar and remaining
cinnamon in a small bowl. Roll biscuits in mixture; arrange in a
greased Bundt® pan. Pour brown sugar mixture over top; bake at
325 degrees for 30 minutes or until golden. Let stand several minutes
before turning out of pan. Serve warm. Makes 10 to 12 servings.

Making salad for a crowd? Wash the greens, tear into bite-size
pieces, wrap in paper towels and place them in large plastic
zipping bags. Refrigerate until serving time. Presto...crisp, dry
greens all ready for dressing!

Blueberry Streusel Muffins

Brenda Hall
Brunswick, OH

These sweet muffins are just right with a cup of tea while chatting with family & friends.

1 c. milk
1/4 c. oil
1/2 t. vanilla extract
1 egg
2-1/4 c. all-purpose flour, divided
1/3 c. sugar

1 T. baking powder
1/2 t. salt
1 c. blueberries
2 T. margarine
2 T. brown sugar, packed
1/4 t. cinnamon

Blend together milk, oil, vanilla and egg. Stir in 2 cups flour, sugar, baking powder and salt. Stir in blueberries. Line muffin tins with paper baking cups; drop batter into cups by tablespoonfuls. Mix together remaining flour, margarine, brown sugar and cinnamon; top each muffin with 2 teaspoons of mixture. Bake at 400 degrees for 20 to 25 minutes. Makes one dozen.

Fill an enamelware pail with crushed ice and everyone's favorite frozen treats...ice pops and ice cream bars. The kids will love it and adults will wonder why it's been so long since they last enjoyed these treats!

Broccoli-Cauliflower Salad

Susie Backus
Gooseberry Patch

*Family & friends always ask me to bring this salad whenever I go
to cookouts or our annual neighborhood block party.*

1 head cauliflower, finely
   chopped
1 bunch broccoli, finely chopped

4-oz. jar real bacon bits
2 c. shredded Cheddar cheese
8-oz. bottle slaw dressing

Combine cauliflower, broccoli, bacon and cheese; pour dressing over
the top. Toss to coat; chill. Serves 10.

A pretty frame for a special photo...pad a simple frame with
quilt batting and cover with fabric from Grandma's sewing
basket. Surround the frame opening with vintage costume
jewelry and fabric flowers. So sweet!

Oriental Slaw Salad

Elaine Miller
Waterville, OH

A buffet favorite! You can use either chicken or Oriental flavor ramen noodles. Serve immediately for crunchy noodles or refrigerate 2 hours or more for a softer texture.

16-oz. pkg. coleslaw mix
1 bunch green onions, chopped
1/2 c. sunflower kernels
1/2 c. sliced almonds
2 3-oz. pkgs. ramen noodles
   with seasoning packets

1 c. oil
1/2 c. sugar
1/3 c. vinegar

Combine slaw, onions, sunflower kernels and almonds in a serving bowl. Crush noodles and add to bowl; set aside. In a small bowl, mix contents of seasoning packets, oil, sugar and vinegar; pour over slaw mixture. Toss to coat; chill. Serves 4 to 6.

Be sure to update family information during your reunion! Set out a sign-up sheet and get everyone's mailing addresses, phone numbers, e-mail addresses, children's names, ages and birthdays. Make copies so everyone can stay in touch.

Calico Beans

Luanne Becker
Manchester, IA

A favorite in my family for many years.

1/2 lb. ground beef
1 onion, diced
1/2 lb. bacon, cut in one-inch
    pieces and crisply cooked
16-oz. can butter beans
16-oz. can kidney beans
20-oz. can pork & beans

1/3 c. brown sugar, packed
1/2 c. sugar
1/4 c. catsup
1/2 t. mustard
2 T. molasses
1/4 t. Worcestershire sauce

Brown ground beef with onion; drain. Place in a 2-quart baking dish; add bacon and beans. Mix well. Stir in remaining ingredients. Bake, uncovered, for one hour at 350 degrees. Serves 8 to 10.

Patchwork Rice

Vickie

Use any colorful seasonal vegetables...broccoli, yellow squash, carrots, celery, cauliflower, green & red peppers.

5 T. butter
1 onion, chopped
4-oz. can sliced mushrooms,
    drained
2-1/2 to 3 c. assorted
    vegetables, chopped

1 to 2 apples, cored and chopped
2 6-oz. pkgs. long grain & wild
    rice mix with seasoning
    packets
4 c. chicken broth

Melt butter in a large saucepan; sauté onion until translucent. Add mushrooms and vegetables; sauté for an additional 8 minutes. Add apple; sauté an additional 2 minutes. Add rice and contents of seasoning packets; mix well and stir in broth. Bring to a boil; cover, reduce heat and simmer until broth is absorbed, 20 to 25 minutes. Serves 6 to 8.

Hail, Hail, the Gang's all Here

Aunt Di's Corn Casserole

Dian Green
Bangs, TX

This is a tradition at our family gatherings.

1 T. butter
8-oz. pkg. cream cheese, cubed
8-oz. pkg. pasteurized processed
   cheese spread, cubed

4-oz. can diced green chiles
2 11-oz. cans corn & diced
   peppers, drained
16-oz. pkg. frozen corn

Microwave butter, cream cheese and processed cheese on high setting for 2 minutes; stir until creamy and smooth. Add chiles, corn & peppers and frozen corn. Heat in microwave on high setting for an additional 5 minutes, stirring occasionally. Makes 8 to 10 servings.

Bubbie's Rice & Noodle Casserole

Lisa Nash
Englewood, CO

We love this yummy dish with baked chicken!

1 c. long-cooking rice, uncooked
1 c. egg noodles, uncooked
4-oz. can mushroom stems,
   drained

1-1/2 oz. pkg. onion soup mix
1/4 c. butter, sliced
4 c. boiling water

Combine rice, noodles, mushroom stems and onion soup mix in a 13"x9" baking dish; dot with butter. Cover with water; bake at 325 degrees for one hour. Serves 8 to 10.

Wind sparkling white lights in your trees or around your patio for a twinkling firefly effect as the sun goes down.

Vegetable Medley

Christina Foster
Kansas City, MO

A delicious, healthy dish for your next potluck. Try adding snow peas or green beans!

2 cloves garlic, minced
1/4 c. olive oil, divided
1 yellow squash, chopped
1 zucchini, chopped
1 green pepper, chopped

1 red pepper, chopped
2 c. mushrooms, quartered
1 c. broccoli, chopped
1 onion, chopped
steak seasoning to taste

Sauté garlic in a large skillet in one tablespoon oil. Add remaining vegetables; toss with remaining oil and sprinkle to taste with steak seasoning. Sauté vegetables to desired crispness, stirring often, about 8 to 10 minutes. Serve warm. Makes 8 to 10 servings.

Have a reunion bonfire in the fall when the weather turns cool & crisp. Hold a weenie roast, add a hearty pot of baked beans, simmering spiced cider to drink and later, s'mores for dessert!

Hail, Hail, the Gang's all Here

Sweet Onion-Swiss Dip

Patricia Nazaruk
Michigan Center, MI

Toasted rounds of French bread are especially good with this dip.

2 c. sweet onions, chopped
2 c. mayonnaise

2 c. shredded Swiss cheese

Mix all ingredients together; spoon into an 8"x8" baking dish. Bake at 375 degrees for 30 minutes or until golden and bubbling. Let cool several minutes before serving. Serves 6 to 8.

Cheddar-Bacon Dip

Gloria Ciecka
Yorktown, VA

This dip is yummy with crackers, chips or veggies.

2 8-oz. pkgs. cream cheese,
    softened
16-oz. pkg. bacon, crisply
    cooked and crumbled
1 bunch green onions, chopped

2 c. sour cream
1/4 c. mayonnaise
1-1/2 c. shredded Cheddar
    cheese

Beat cream cheese until smooth; add remaining ingredients and mix well. Spread in a 9" deep-dish pie plate. Bake at 350 degrees for 20 minutes; let stand for 10 minutes. Serves 6 to 8.

Scooped-out red and yellow peppers make fun containers for dips and sauces.

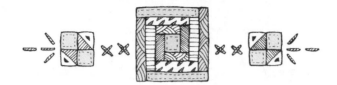

Gooey Buns

Laurie Wilson
Fort Wayne, IN

My mom used to make a lot of these on winter nights. We would enjoy them by the fireplace with family & friends. This recipe is great for large gatherings or potlucks any time of year, though! It can be doubled and the sandwiches frozen and reheated later.

1 lb. bologna
3/4 lb. pasteurized processed
   cheese spread
4 to 5 T. onion, minced
1/4 c. mustard

1/4 c. sweet pickle relish
1/3 c. mayonnaise-type salad
   dressing
20 to 30 hot dog buns

Grind meat and cheese together using a food grinder or food processor. Add remaining ingredients and mix well. Spread lightly on buns; wrap each bun in foil and arrange on baking sheet. Bake at 350 degrees for 25 to 30 minutes. Makes 20 to 30 sandwiches.

Make an ice bowl for your buffet table. Use tape to suspend a small plastic bowl inside a larger one. Fill the space in between with cut flowers, herbs and water and freeze until solid. Gently remove both bowls and fill with fresh fruit. So pretty!

Hail, Hail, the Gang's all Here

Grandma's Sandwiches

Carol Bull
Delaware, OH

A hearty, filling open-face sandwich...so easy to make for a crowd!

8-oz. pkg. pasteurized processed
    cheese spread, cubed
6 eggs, hard-boiled, peeled and
    finely chopped
12-oz. bottle chili sauce
2 onions, finely chopped

8 to 12 slices bacon, crisply
    cooked and crumbled
4-oz. jar pimentos, drained and
    chopped
6 to 8 English muffins, split

Mix all ingredients except muffins in a large bowl. Pile mixture on split muffins; arrange on a baking sheet. Broil until bubbly and golden. Makes 12 to 16.

Be sure to label your photos with names, places and dates.
If you have "mystery" photos, bring them to family reunions
for help in identifying the folks in the photos.

Hoosier Grilled Tenderloin

Teresa Stiegelmeyer
Indianapolis, IN

Our teenage boys love this…it's always a favorite for barbecues. Any leftovers make great sandwiches!

7-lb. beef tenderloin
1/2 c. butter, melted and cooled
8-oz. bottle Italian salad
    dressing

4-oz. jar minced garlic
12-oz. bottle dark molasses,
    divided

Place beef in a large plastic zipping bag; set aside. Combine butter, salad dressing and garlic; pour over beef and refrigerate overnight. Remove beef from bag; discard marinade. Brush beef with molasses and place on a preheated grill. Brush with molasses 2 to 3 times during grilling. Grill over medium high heat for 4 to 6 minutes on each side or to desired doneness. Slice to serve. Serves 6 to 8.

Grilled Parmesan Potatoes

Paula Smith
Ottawa, IL

A cookout favorite…equally good oven-baked at 350 degrees.

6 potatoes, peeled and thinly
    sliced
1 onion, thinly sliced
1/2 c. grated Parmesan cheese

2 cloves garlic, minced
4 T. butter, cubed
1 t. seasoning salt
1/2 t. pepper

Layer 2 pieces of aluminum foil about 20 inches long. Combine all ingredients in a bowl; mix well. Place potato mixture in the center of the aluminum foil; fold foil up around potatoes and seal. Grill, covered, over medium heat for 30 to 40 minutes, or until potatoes are tender. Serves 6.

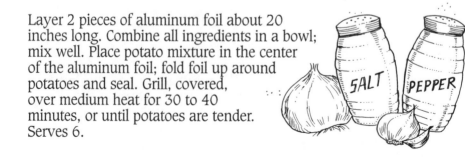

Hail, Hail, the Gang's all Here

Grandma's Meatballs & Sauce

Devona Casto
Liberty, WV

Great for meatball sandwiches on crusty hard rolls or served with buttery mashed potatoes.

1 lb. ground beef
5-oz. can evaporated milk
1/2 c. onion, chopped
3/4 c. quick-cooking oats,
    uncooked
salt and pepper to taste

1 c. catsup
2 T. Worcestershire sauce
2 T. brown sugar, packed
1 T. vinegar
1/2 c. water

Mix together ground beef, evaporated milk, onion, oats, salt and pepper; roll into one-inch balls. Brown in a skillet for 2 to 4 minutes; place in a 13"x9" baking pan. Set aside. Combine catsup, Worcestershire sauce, sugar, vinegar and water; pour over meatballs. Bake at 350 degrees for one hour. Makes about one dozen.

T-shirts are a fun memento for family reunions. Get the computer-savvy teens in your family to design iron-on transfers for your shirts.

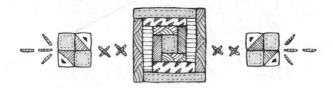

Hawaiian Pizza Sub

Mary Patenaude
Griswold, CT

*A scrumptious blend of flavors, made even better by
fresh-baked bread!*

11-oz. tube refrigerated crusty
   French loaf dough
2 T. oil
1 t. Italian seasoning
1/4 t. garlic salt

8-oz. can pizza sauce, divided
1/3 lb. sliced deli ham
8-oz. can crushed pineapple,
   drained
1 c. shredded mozzarella cheese

Place loaf seam-side down on a greased baking sheet; cut slashes about 1/2 inch deep on top. Bake at 350 degrees for 25 to 30 minutes, or until golden; remove from oven and set aside. Combine oil, Italian seasoning and garlic salt in a small bowl; brush over hot loaf. Cool for 10 minutes; split loaf in half lengthwise. Hollow out bottom half of the loaf, leaving a 1/4-inch shell; spread with 2 tablespoons of the pizza sauce. Top with ham, pineapple and cheese; replace top of loaf. Return to oven for an additional 6 to 8 minutes. Slice and serve with remaining pizza sauce. Serves 4 to 6.

A festive container for chips or snack mix on a potluck table...simply tie a knot in each corner of a bandanna, then tuck a bowl of goodies into the center.

Pizza Burgers

Marsha Waldron
Little Rock, AR

Kids just love these tasty little pizzas!

2 lbs. ground beef
1/2 green pepper, diced
1 onion, diced
2 T. sugar
26-oz. can spaghetti sauce with
    mushrooms

6-oz. can tomato paste
1 doz. hamburger buns, split
2 c. shredded mozzarella cheese
1/2 c. grated Parmesan cheese

Brown ground beef with pepper, onion and sugar in a skillet; drain and set aside. Mix spaghetti sauce with tomato paste; stir into beef mixture. Spread on each bun half; sprinkle with cheeses. Arrange on ungreased baking sheets. Bake at 500 degrees for 5 minutes. Makes 2 dozen.

Want to capture all the guests at your reunion on film, but there are just too many to fit into one photo? Pick up a disposable "panorama" style camera...room for everyone!

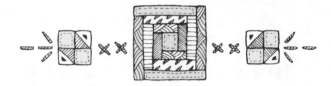

Quilters' Brew

Cheryl Chapman
Union, MO

We enjoy this beverage whenever my quilting club gets together.

11 c. water, divided
9 teabags
12 to 14 whole allspice
8 whole cloves
zest of 1/2 orange

12-oz. can frozen orange juice
   concentrate
1/2 c. lemon juice
1/2 c. sugar
1/4 c. honey

Pour 9 cups water into a large stockpot. Add teabags, allspice, cloves and orange zest; simmer until desired strength is reached. Strain. Add remaining 2 cups water, orange juice, lemon juice, sugar and honey to mixture; stir and heat through. Makes 13 to 15 servings.

A punch bowl is a festive touch that makes even the simplest beverage special! Surround it with a simple wreath of fresh flowers or even bunches of grapes.

Hail, Hail, the Gang's all Here

Sweet Citrus Cooler

Melissa Berlin
Titusville, PA

This sweet, tangy beverage will really "hit the spot" at warm weather get-togethers!

juice of 5 lemons
juice of 5 limes
juice of 5 oranges
3 qts. cold water

1-1/2 to 2 c. sugar
2 T. hot water
Garnish: citrus slices

Combine juices in a one-gallon pitcher; add cold water and stir. Dissolve sugar in hot water; add to juice mixture and mix well. Chill; serve over ice. Garnish glasses with slices of lemon, lime or orange. Makes 3 to 3-1/2 quarts.

Grandma's wicker laundry basket makes a handy tote for backyard play equipment...volleyball, badminton and the kids' bouncy balls.

Spinach-Artichoke Dip

Carol Beck
Columbia, IL

A great party dip that we all love with tortilla chips or crackers.

14-oz. can artichoke hearts,
   drained and chopped
10-oz. pkg. frozen chopped
   spinach, thawed and drained
1 to 2 c. mayonnaise

1 c. shredded mozzarella cheese
1 c. grated Parmesan cheese
1 clove garlic, pressed
Optional: roasted red pepper or
   green onion, chopped

Combine artichokes, spinach, mayonnaise, cheeses and garlic. Mix well and spread in a 13"x9" baking dish. Sprinkle with red pepper or green onion, if desired. Bake at 325 degrees for 20 to 30 minutes, until heated through, bubbly, and top is golden. Serves 10 to 12.

Instant lawn bowling fun for the kids! Fill
10 matching plastic soda bottles with water and
set up in a triangle. Use a softball or croquet ball...let 'er roll!

Hail, Hail, the Gang's all Here

Peppery Dip

Dale-Harriet Rogovich
Madison, WI

*This delicious dip could not be easier! If you can't find the pepper
sauce, a sweet steak sauce is a good substitute.*

8-oz. pkg. cream cheese,
  softened
1/2 c. Jamaican pepper sauce

water crackers or round buttery
crackers

Unwrap cream cheese and place on a serving plate. Pour pepper sauce
over the cheese; surround with crackers. Makes 4 to 6 servings.

Reunions are a wonderful time for storytelling
and chatting about family history. Be sure to include
the older kids!

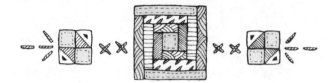

Ginger Wings

Kristin Winterhoff
Jersey City, NJ

My mother brought home this recipe from a card party...they are the best wings you will ever eat!

1/2 c. soy sauce
1 c. brown sugar, packed
1/2-inch slice fresh ginger,
   peeled and shredded

4 to 5 cloves garlic, pressed
1 to 2 T. oil
5 lbs. chicken wings

Mix together all ingredients except wings; pour over wings in a large container. Cover and refrigerate all day, stirring occasionally. Arrange on jelly-roll pans. Bake at 450 degrees for one hour, turning frequently. Makes about 4 dozen.

Have everyone bring old home movies and videos to your reunion. The kids will giggle when they see their parents as children and you'll be ready with a rainy-day activity. Remember to provide plenty of popcorn and floor pillows!

Crabbies

Susan Ruff
Dayton, OH

My family & friends always request these tasty tidbits at get-togethers. This is a great make-ahead recipe...pop under the broiler just before serving time!

1/2 c. butter, softened
5-oz. jar sharp pasteurized
   process cheese spread,
   softened
1-1/2 t. mayonnaise

1/2 t. garlic salt
1/2 t. seasoned salt
7-oz. can crabmeat, drained
6 English muffins, split

Blend the first 6 ingredients together; spread on muffin halves. Cut each half into 6 wedges; arrange on an ungreased baking sheet. Broil until bubbly. Makes 6 dozen.

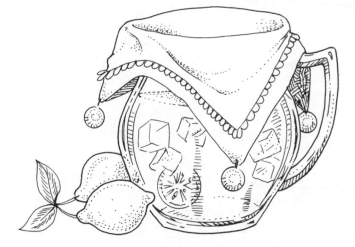

Keep flying insects out of your picnic beverages...just stitch 4 large beads or pretty seashells to the corners of a table napkin and drape over your open pitcher.

Patchwork Crafts

Make a new quilt

Make a keepsake quilt for a bridal or anniversary gift. Ask everyone to contribute a decorated fabric square, using fabric crayons or pens, iron-on photo transfers, embroidery, buttons and beads.

Make an endearing lap quilt for Grandma. Cut squares from grandchildren's favorite outgrown clothing.

Make a throw from Grandma's hankie collection. Arrange and stitch onto solid-color cloth, in rows or in a random arrangement.

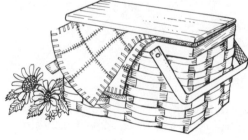

Make a rag quilt from old denim jeans...sturdy enough for picnics and trips to the beach.

To finish...layer quilt batting with a backing of solid color or fun fabric print. Tack with yarn, thin ribbon or vintage buttons.

Patchwork Crafts

Give new meaning to an old, worn quilt

Turn still good portions into:

◉ A pillow top for a ready-made pillow

◉ A table runner

◉ A Christmas tree skirt

◉ A tea cozy

◉ A doll's quilt

◉ A simple stuffed toy

◉ A mat for a family photo

Patchwork Crafts

Grandma's Button Jar

Button, button, who's got the button?

Sweater
Replace all the buttons on a favorite cardigan with interesting mismatched buttons.

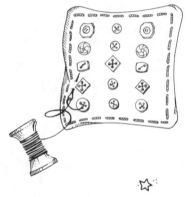

Pillow
Stitch rows of vintage buttons across a ready-made pillow.

Lamp
Make a lamp of a button-filled jar, using a simple kit from a craft store...you don't even have to drill the jar. Glue more buttons onto lampshade in patterns or completely cover the shade with buttons.

Napkin rings
So easy! Just string together buttons on an elastic cord.

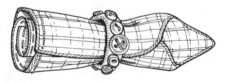

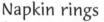

Grandma's Bringing Dessert

Old-fashioned treats

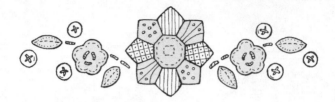

Grandma Tille's Cookies

Roberta McCarthy
Reinbeck, IA

My grandmother always made sure to bake our favorite cookies when we visited. Before we even opened the door, we could smell the sweet aroma of molasses and cinnamon coming from her kitchen.

2 T. baking soda
3/4 c. milk, divided
3-1/2 c. sugar
1-1/2 c. margarine, softened
2 c. raisins, finely chopped
1 T. salt
1/2 c. molasses

4 t. cinnamon
4 c. quick-cooking oats, uncooked
1 T. vanilla extract
3 eggs, divided
6 c. all-purpose flour

Dissolve baking soda in 1/2 cup milk. Combine with sugar, margarine, raisins, salt, molasses, cinnamon, oats, vanilla, 2 eggs and flour. Mix well; roll out on lightly floured surface to 1/2-inch thick. Stir together remaining egg and milk; brush over dough. Cut into 3"x4" rectangles using a knife or pizza cutter. Arrange on ungreased baking sheets; bake at 375 degrees for 12 to 15 minutes. Makes 4 dozen.

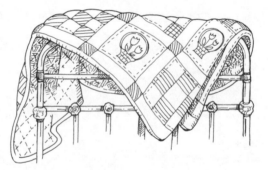

Of all the things a woman's hands have made,
The quilt so lightly thrown across her bed -
The quilt that keeps her loved ones warm -
Is woven of her love and dreams and thread.

-Carrie A. Hall

Grandma's Bringing Dessert

Mom & Me Peanut Butter Kisses

Nicole Wrigley
Vancouver, WA

My mom and I first made these for the holidays...but they were so good, we make them year 'round now!

1 c. creamy peanut butter
1 c. sugar
1 egg

24 milk chocolate drops, unwrapped

Combine peanut butter, sugar and egg in a bowl; mix well. Roll into small balls and arrange on an ungreased baking sheet. Bake at 350 degrees for 12 minutes. Remove from oven; immediately place a chocolate drop in the center of each cookie. Makes about 2 dozen.

Set out whipped cream and shakers of cinnamon and cocoa at dessert time for coffee-drinkers. Tea drinkers will love a basket of special teas with honey and lemon slices. Grandma's desserts deserve the best!

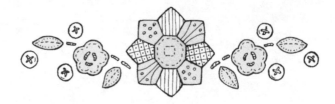

Graham Cracker Pudding

Kathi Zerkle
Saint Paris, OH

When I was a child, any day was special when my mother made this dessert. Now I make it for my own children.

1-1/4 c. graham cracker crumbs
1/3 c. butter, melted
1-1/4 c. sugar, divided
6 T. all-purpose flour
2 eggs, separated and divided

1 qt. milk
1 t. vanilla extract
Optional: extra graham cracker
    crumbs

Combine cracker crumbs, butter and 1/4 cup sugar; mix well. Press into a 2-quart baking dish; set aside. Blend remaining sugar, flour, egg yolks and milk in a saucepan; heat until mixture thickens. Stir in vanilla; pour over crumb mixture. Beat egg whites until stiff; spread over filling. Sprinkle with additional graham cracker crumbs, if desired. Bake at 350 degrees for 15 minutes. Serves 6 to 8.

Welcome a new bride into the family with copies
of her new hubby's best childhood photos! Add amusing
and heartfelt captions and tuck into a small
photo album.

Grandma's Bringing
❀ Dessert ❀

Mississippi Dirt Pudding

Rob McKelvy
Roswell, NM

Kids and adults alike are amused by this pudding! Just for fun, make it in a clean new flower pot, poke in a plastic flower and serve with a new trowel.

1/4 c. butter, softened
8-oz. pkg. cream cheese,
　softened
1 c. powdered sugar
3-1/2 c. milk
2 5-1/4 oz. pkgs. instant vanilla
　pudding mix

12-oz. container frozen whipped
　topping, thawed
20-oz. pkg. chocolate sandwich
　cookies, crushed
Optional: gummy worms

Combine butter and cream cheese; mix until creamy. Stir in powdered sugar, milk, and pudding mix; beat well. Fold in whipped topping. Layer one-third of the cookie crumbs in the bottom of a 13"x9" baking dish. Top with half of the pudding mixture, another layer of crumbs, the remaining pudding and the remaining crumbs. Refrigerate 2 hours to overnight. Garnish with gummy worms, if desired. Makes 8 to 10 servings.

Hand down a special item from Grandma's kitchen as a bridal shower gift...a teapot stuffed with teabags, a cookie jar filled with cookie cutters. Tuck in a favorite recipe too!

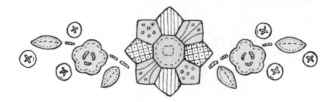

Strawberry-Pecan Crunch

Melissa Ward
Ila, GA

This is my husband's absolute favorite dessert. His favorite aunt used to make it for him. He still requests it for his birthday!

1 egg
1 c. sugar
1 c. chopped pecans
2 c. strawberries, hulled and
    sliced
1 c. milk

8-oz. container frozen whipped
    topping, thawed
3.9-oz. pkg. instant vanilla
    pudding mix
1 c. sour cream

Line a baking sheet with aluminum foil and spray with non-stick vegetable spray; set aside. Blend together egg and sugar; stir in pecans. Pour into the center of prepared baking sheet. Bake at 350 degrees for 15 minutes. Let cool; crumble half of mixture into a 13"x9" baking dish. Arrange strawberries over pecan mixture; set aside. Combine milk, whipped topping, pudding mix and sour cream; mix well. Pour over strawberries; top with reserved pecan mixture. Chill before serving. Serves 6 to 8.

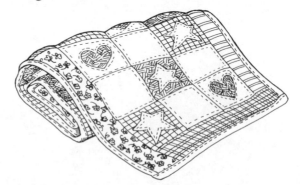

You inherited a family quilt...how lucky! Preserve it for future generations by handling as little as possible. Don't wash or dry clean; if it needs freshening, simply air in the shade on a clean sheet, or gently clean with a hand-held vacuum. Display your quilt draped over a quilt rack or a guest-room bed, in a dry area away from strong light.

Grandma's Cherry Cobbler

Kathy Moser
Allison, PA

It's always a favorite at our family reunions...so simple and good. It's yummy made with crushed pineapple instead of cherry pie filling too.

1 c. margarine, softened	1 t. vanilla extract
1 c. sugar	2 c. all-purpose flour
2 eggs	21-oz. can cherry pie filling

Blend together margarine and sugar until creamy; stir in eggs and vanilla. Add flour; blend well. Spread half of mixture in an ungreased 10"x6" baking pan. Spread cherry filling on top. Drop remaining mixture by teaspoonfuls on top of filling; carefully spread it out a little. Bake at 350 degrees for 30 to 40 minutes until golden, checking after 30 minutes to avoid browning. Serves 6 to 8.

Invite friends to an ice cream social! Set out big tubs of ice cream in yummy flavors, plus all the toppings we love...hot fudge, nuts, chopped candy bars, jimmies and whipped cream. Don't forget the maraschino cherries!

German Chocolate Upside-Down Cake
Janice White
Knoxville, TN

My Aunt Mary gave me the recipe for this moist, rich cake that she always made for our family reunions and special gatherings.

1/2 c. chopped pecans
7-oz. pkg. flaked coconut
18-1/4 oz. pkg. German
   chocolate cake mix

1/2 c. butter, softened
8-oz. pkg. cream cheese,
   softened
16-oz. pkg. powdered sugar

Mix pecans and coconut; spread in bottom of a greased 13"x9" baking dish. Prepare cake mix according to package directions; pour batter into baking pan. Blend butter and cream cheese in a large mixing bowl, adding powdered sugar slowly, until smooth and creamy. Spoon mixture on top of cake. Bake at 300 degrees for one hour. Serves 10 to 12.

Every day of our lives we make deposits in the memory banks of our children.

-Charles R. Swindoll

Grandma's Bringing
🌸 Dessert 🌸

Grandma Rene's Crumb Cake

Jacquelynn Daunce
Lockport, NY

My 3 brothers and I couldn't wait to see our Grandma Rene when she came every Sunday for dinner! She always brought along this cake for dessert. The banana makes it nice and moist.

2 c. brown sugar, packed
2 c. all-purpose flour
1 c. butter, softened
1 t. baking soda
1 t. salt
1 c. milk
1 t. vanilla extract

1 t. cinnamon
1/2 t. ground cloves
1/2 t. nutmeg
1 banana, mashed
1/2 c. chopped walnuts
1/2 c. raisins
Optional: whipped cream

Combine brown sugar and flour in a large bowl; set aside 1/2 cup of mixture for crumb topping. Blend butter into remaining flour mixture. Stir baking soda and salt into milk. Add milk, vanilla, spices, banana, nuts and raisins to flour mixture. Mix well until batter is slightly lumpy. Pour batter into a greased 13"x9" baking pan. Sprinkle with reserved crumb topping; do not stir. Bake at 350 degrees for 45 minutes until dark golden. Top with whipped cream, if desired. Makes 10 to 12 servings.

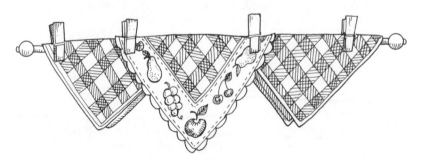

Grandma's flowery tea towels make precious window valances...just drape over the curtain rod. For longer curtains, try hanging small fruit-printed tablecloths with clip hooks. So cheerful!

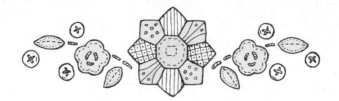

Peppermint Ice Cream

Belinda Meador
Sweeny, TX

This is a 4th of July tradition in my family. It's my father's favorite...one year he cut his vacation short so he wouldn't miss it!

4 eggs, beaten
1 c. sugar
1 c. whipping cream
4 c. milk, divided

10-oz. pkg. mini marshmallows
12-oz. pkg. peppermint candies, crushed

Combine eggs, sugar, whipping cream and 2 cups milk. Add marshmallows and candies. Pour into a saucepan; heat over low heat until marshmallows and candies are melted. Stirring constantly, add remaining milk. Pour into an electric ice cream maker; freeze according to manufacturer's instructions. Serves 10 to 12.

Chocolate Frostie Ice Cream

Kimberly Bowersox
Morristown, TN

Such a simple, delicious recipe for chocolate ice cream!

1/2 gal. chocolate whole milk
12-oz. container frozen whipped topping, thawed

14-oz. can sweetened condensed milk

Combine all ingredients; mix well. Pour into an electric ice cream maker; freeze according to manufacturer's instructions. Serves 16 to 20.

Grandma's Bringing
❀ Dessert ❀

Snow Creme

Beverly Whedbee
Chesapeake, VA

This tastes just like homemade ice cream and freezes well.
We've enjoyed it from the freezer as late as June.

14-oz. can sweetened condensed
   milk

3 qt. freshly fallen snow
1 T. vanilla extract

Blend condensed milk into snow; add vanilla and mix until creamy.
Serve immediately or store in freezer. Makes 4 to 6 servings.

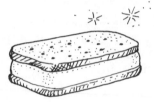

Ice Cream Sandwiches

Shari Miller
Hobart, IN

Keep these in your freezer for those hot summer days when
the kids want a treat!

3.4-oz. pkg. instant vanilla
   pudding mix
2 c. milk
2 c. frozen whipped topping,
   thawed

1 c. semi-sweet mini chocolate
   chips
24 graham crackers, halved

Mix pudding and milk according to package directions; refrigerate
until set. Fold in whipped topping and chocolate chips. Arrange
24 graham cracker halves on a baking sheet; top each with with
about 3 tablespoons of filling. Top each with another graham cracker
half. Wrap individually in plastic wrap. Freeze for one hour or until
firm. Makes 2 dozen.

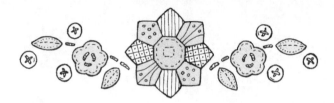

Cora's Jam Cake

Carma Brown
Xenia, OH

My grandmother had this recipe written down in a notebook dated 1941.

2-1/2 c. all-purpose flour
2/3 c. margarine, melted
1 c. seedless blackberry jam
2/3 c. sour cream
2 eggs, beaten
1 c. sugar

1 t. baking soda
1 t. ground cloves
1 t. cinnamon
1 t. allspice
1 t. nutmeg

Combine all ingredients in a large bowl; mix well. Pour into greased and floured 13"x9" baking pan. Bake at 350 degrees for 25 minutes or until toothpick inserted in center of cake comes out clean. Cool; spread with caramel frosting. Serves 6 to 8.

Caramel Frosting:

1/2 c. butter
1 c. brown sugar, packed

1/4 c. milk
2 c. powdered sugar

Melt butter in a saucepan. Add brown sugar and milk; heat over low heat. Add powdered sugar, beating well after each addition until thick enough to spread.

Restore Grandma's treasured silver to its gleaming glory with...toothpaste! Simply use white paste-style (not gel) toothpaste and a soft old toothbrush to brush away tarnish. Rinse with warm water and polish with a soft cloth. Beautiful!

Wild Blueberry Cake

*Faith Frattasio
Pembroke, MA*

I won a blue ribbon at a local fair with my grandmother's recipe.

3 c. all-purpose flour
2-1/2 c. sugar, divided
1 T. baking powder
1 t. salt
2 eggs

1/3 c. oil
1 c. milk
1/2 t. vanilla extract
2 c. blueberries
3/4 t. nutmeg

Combine flour, 2 cups sugar, baking powder and salt in a large bowl. Add eggs, oil, milk and vanilla; mix well. Fold in blueberries; pour into a greased and floured 13"x9" baking pan and set aside. Combine remaining sugar and nutmeg; sprinkle over batter. Bake at 350 degrees for 50 minutes. Serves 6 to 8.

Vintage cigar boxes were always too nice to throw away...Grandpa probably had a closet full of them. Your kids will love 'em for keeping secret treasures.

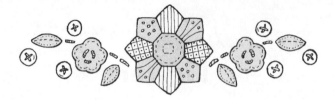

Peanut Butter Candy

Deborah Hiatt
Mount Airy, NC

My mama made this for my brothers, sisters and me as a rare treat.

1/4 c. margarine, melted
3 to 4 c. powdered sugar

2 to 4 T. evaporated milk
1/4 c. creamy peanut butter

Combine margarine and sugar in a bowl. Stir in 2 tablespoons milk until mixture is stiff, adding more milk as necessary. Divide into 3 parts; roll each part out into a circle on a flat surface lightly sprinkled with powdered sugar. Spread equal amounts of peanut butter on each circle. Roll up each circle jelly-roll style; arrange on a baking sheet. Refrigerate, covered, for 30 minutes. Slice each roll into one-inch pieces. Makes about 15 to 20 pieces.

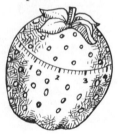

White Chocolate Fudge

Sharon Crider
Lebanon, MO

A delicious, easy-to-make candy.

8-oz. pkg. cream cheese, softened
4 c. powdered sugar
1-1/2 t. vanilla extract

12-oz. pkg. white chocolate chips
3/4 c. chopped pecans

Blend cream cheese, sugar and vanilla until smooth; set aside. Melt chocolate in a double boiler over hot water; fold into cream cheese mixture with pecans. Spread in a lightly buttered 8"x8" baking pan. Chill until ready to serve. Makes 2 dozen pieces.

Grandma's Bringing
❀ **Dessert** ❀

Mother's Chocolate Fudge

Lillian Westfelt
Loveland, OH

Get a friend to help you beat this fudge...for a homemade fudge that just can't be beat!

2 c. sugar
5-oz. can evaporated milk
1/3 c. baking cocoa
1/4 t. salt

2 T. light corn syrup
2 T. butter
1 t. vanilla extract
1/2 c. chopped pecans

Combine sugar, evaporated milk, cocoa, salt and corn syrup in a large saucepan over medium heat. Stir constantly until sugar dissolves and mixture reaches soft-ball stage, or 234 to 243 degrees on a candy thermometer. Remove saucepan from heat and place in a pan of cold water. Add butter and vanilla; do not stir. Allow mixture to cool until lukewarm, 30 to 40 minutes. Beat by hand with a wooden spoon for 5 to 10 minutes until fudge is thick and loses its gloss. Stir in nuts and immediately spread in a buttered 8"x8" serving dish; chill. Makes about 16 pieces.

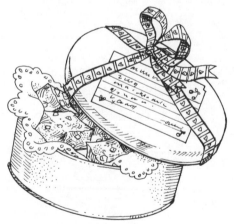

Decoupage Mom's favorite cookie or candy recipe onto the lid of a tin, then line with a lacy napkin...a thoughtful container for delivering goodies to a lucky friend or relative.

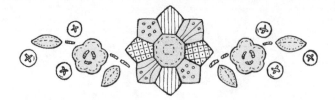

Grandma's Grange Cookies

Vivien Mullins
Hilliard, OH

A family favorite that my Grandmother Monnie used to make.
Sometimes we like to tint the frosting with food coloring.

2/3 c. butter, softened
1-1/2 c. brown sugar, packed
2 eggs
1 t. vanilla extract
1 t. vinegar

1 c. evaporated milk
2-1/2 to 3 c. all-purpose flour
1 t. baking soda
1/2 t. baking powder

Blend butter and brown sugar in a bowl; add eggs, vanilla, vinegar
and milk. Mix well and set aside. Sift together flour, baking soda and
baking powder; add to butter mixture. Drop by tablespoonfuls onto an
ungreased baking sheet; bake at 350 degrees for 10 to 12 minutes
until golden. Cool and frost. Makes about 2 dozen.

Frosting:

1/2 c. butter
1/4 c. boiling water

3 c. powdered sugar

Melt butter in a small saucepan; add water and pour over powdered
sugar in a mixing bowl. Stir until thick.

I am still convinced that a good, simple, homemade cookie is
preferable to all the store-bought cookies one can find.

-James Beard

Chocolate Chip-Raisin Cookies

*Amy Ceaser
York, PA*

*My grandmother's down-home cooking was the best...this recipe
is a treasured memory of her.*

2 c. raisins	1 t. baking powder
2 c. water	1 t. baking soda
1 c. lard or shortening	1 t. salt
2 c. sugar	1/2 t. nutmeg
3 eggs, beaten	1 t. cinnamon
1 t. vanilla extract	1/4 t. allspice
4 c. all-purpose flour	12-oz. pkg. chocolate chips

Simmer raisins in water for 5 minutes; do not drain. Set aside to cool.
Blend together lard or shortening, sugar, eggs and vanilla; add raisins
and water. Sift together flour, baking powder, baking soda, salt and
spices; slowly mix into shortening mixture. Add chocolate chips; drop
by tablespoonfuls onto a greased baking sheet. Bake at 375 degrees
until golden, about 10 minutes. Makes 2-1/2 to 3 dozen.

Be sure to ask your kids about their favorite foods,
if you're compiling a family cookbook. You may find you
have "traditions" in your own family that you
weren't even aware of!

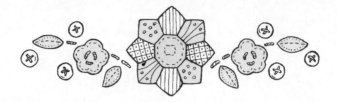

Lemon Sponge Pie

Rebecca Bressan
Pullman, WA

This is one of my Great-Grandmother Morgan's kitchen creations...a delicious lemon pie that resembles a sponge cake and has a delightful lemon surprise with each bite.

1 c. sugar
3 T. butter, softened
3 eggs, separated and divided
3 T. lemon juice

zest of one lemon
3 T. all-purpose flour
1 c. milk
9-inch pie crust

Combine sugar, butter and egg yolks; add lemon juice and zest. Add flour and milk; mix well. Fold in stiffly beaten egg whites; mix gently. Pour into pie crust; bake uncovered at 425 degrees for 15 minutes. Reduce to 375 degrees and bake for an additional 30 minutes or until golden. Serves 6 to 8.

Dress up a cake with edible flowers...roses, nasturtiums, violets and pansies are all pretty choices. Make sure your flowers are pesticide-free and wash them well before using.

Grandma's Bringing
✺ Dessert ✺

Granny's Apple Coffee Cake

Phyllis Cowgill
LaPorte, IN

I remember my mother and great-grandmother making this cake with apples and butternuts picked right off the tree and fresh milk from our cows. It's good on a cold brisk morning with a cup of coffee.

3/4 c. sugar
1-1/2 c. all-purpose flour
2 t. baking powder
1/4 t. salt
1 t. cinnamon

1/2 c. margarine, softened
2 eggs
3/4 c. milk
2-1/4 c. apples, cored, peeled, sliced and divided

Combine sugar, flour, baking powder, salt and cinnamon in a bowl; mix well. Blend in margarine, eggs and milk; pour half of batter into a greased and floured 9"x9" baking pan. Arrange half of apples over batter; sprinkle with half of the topping. Arrange remaining apples over topping, followed by remaining batter and remaining topping. Bake at 350 degrees for 40 minutes. Makes 16 servings.

Topping:

1/2 c. brown sugar, packed
3 T. all-purpose flour
1/2 c. chopped walnuts

1-1/2 t. cinnamon
1 T. margarine

Combine all ingredients in a bowl; mix well.

Bring out Grandma's cheery fruit or flower table linens for special family get-togethers...they will spark conversations about other special gatherings.

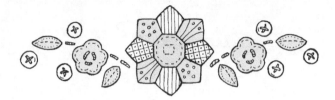

Chocolate Heaven

Christy Kerns
Henderson, WV

A triple delight for chocolate lovers!

18-1/4 oz. pkg. devil's food
  cake mix
2 16-oz. pkgs. caramels,
  unwrapped and melted
2 12-oz. pkgs. peanut butter
  chips, separated

16-oz. container frozen
  whipped topping, thawed
  and separated
2 12-oz. pkgs. chocolate chips,
  separated

Bake cake as package directs; cool completely. Cut into bite-size cubes and arrange in bottom of trifle cake bowl. Spread half of melted caramels over cake; sprinkle with one package peanut butter chips. Spread half of whipped topping over peanut butter chips; sprinkle with one package chocolate chips. Repeat layers of caramels, peanut butter chips, whipped topping and chocolate chips. Makes 10 to 15 servings.

Completing a new quilt...preserving an antique one?
Remember to label it with the quilter's name and
year of completion. Use a fabric pen to write on a
muslin square, then stitch it to the quilt back.
Future owners will thank you for your thoughtfulness.

Mother's Brown Sugar Pudding

Brenda Doak
Gooseberry Patch

When I was a young newlywed many years ago, this was one of the very first of my mother-in-law's recipes that I tried. I usually had all the ingredients on hand and it was so easy and so good. A bit of dessert without much work!

1 c. brown sugar, packed
2 c. hot water
2 T. butter
1/2 c. sugar

1 c. all-purpose flour
2 t. baking powder
1/2 c. milk
Optional: 1/2 c. raisins

Combine brown sugar and water in a saucepan. Heat until boiling; stir in butter and set aside. Sift together sugar, flour and baking powder; add milk and raisins, if desired. Mix well but do not beat mixture. Pour brown sugar mixture into an 8"x8" glass baking dish. Drop batter by spoonfuls onto brown sugar mixture; do not stir. Bake at 350 degrees for 20 to 25 minutes. Serves 9.

Grandma's well-loved cookie cutters hold too many happy
memories to be hidden in a drawer. Tie them to a
grapevine wreath and add a big gingham bow
for a delightful kitchen decoration.

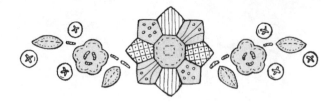

Maple Syrup Cake

Glinda Solomon
Marshall, TX

My mother was raised on this cake...it's easy and very good.

2 eggs
1/2 c. sugar
1/2 c. margarine, softened
1 t. baking soda
1/2 c. buttermilk

2-1/2 c. all-purpose flour
1/4 t. salt
1 c. maple-flavored syrup
1 t. vanilla extract

Combine eggs, sugar and margarine; blend well. Mix in baking soda, buttermilk, flour and salt. Add syrup and vanilla; stir well. Pour into a greased and floured 13"x9" baking pan; bake at 350 degrees for 25 minutes. Cut into squares. Serves 24.

Bring out all the family photo albums for your reunion...sure to spark conversation as your guests look at pictures they haven't seen in years!

Grandma's Bringing
❀ Dessert ❀

Old-Fashioned Shortcake

Nancy Molldrem
Eau Claire, WI

Strawberry shortcake is traditional, but other ripe, juicy fruits like peaches and blueberries make tasty shortcake too!

4 c. all-purpose flour
1 t. salt
1/4 c. sugar
2 T. plus 2 t. baking powder

6 T. shortening
1-1/2 c. milk
Garnish: butter, strawberries,
    whipped cream

Sift together dry ingredients in a mixing bowl; add shortening and enough milk to make a soft dough. Spread in a greased 13"x9" baking pan. Bake at 350 degrees for 20 to 25 minutes until golden. Cool; cut into squares. To serve, split open each square; spread bottom halves lightly with butter. Top with strawberries and whipped cream; add top halves. Makes 8 to 10 servings.

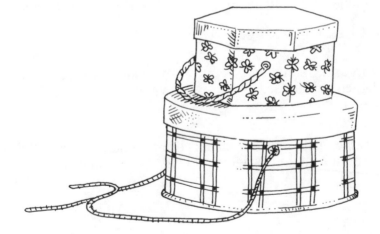

Thrifty grandmothers never threw away extra rolls of wallpaper. Use them to cover a hatbox or 2...clever storage that will bring memories of Grandma's parlor or dining room.

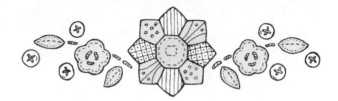

Mom's Hummingbird Cake

Laurie Wilson
Fort Wayne, IN

My mom used to make this scrumptious cake for me...its flavor is outstanding. Thanks for the memories, Mom!

3 c. all-purpose flour
2 c. sugar
1 t. baking soda
1/2 t. salt
1 t. cinnamon
3 eggs, beaten

3/4 c. oil
1-1/2 t. vanilla extract
8-oz. can crushed pineapple
1-3/4 c. bananas, mashed
1-1/2 c. chopped pecans, divided

Combine flour, sugar, baking soda, salt and cinnamon. Add eggs and oil; stir just until dry ingredients are moistened. Stir in vanilla, pineapple, bananas and one cup pecans. Pour into 3 greased and floured 9" round cake pans. Bake at 350 degrees for 25 to 30 minutes. Cool in pans for 10 minutes; remove from pans and let cool completely. Spread frosting between layers and on top and sides of cake. Sprinkle remaining pecans on top. Makes 8 to 10 servings.

Cream Cheese Frosting:

1/2 c. margarine, softened
8-oz. pkg. cream cheese,
    softened

16-oz. pkg. powdered sugar
1 t. vanilla extract

Blend together margarine and cream cheese. Gradually add powdered sugar; beat until mixture is light and fluffy. Stir in vanilla.

Mum's Tomato Soup Cake

Lisa Meyerhuber
Apollo, PA

People are always so surprised when you tell them what this spice cake's secret ingredient is!

2 c. sugar
1/4 c. shortening
10-3/4 oz. can tomato soup
1 t. baking soda
2 t. baking powder

2 t. cinnamon
1 t. ground cloves
1/4 t. allspice
4 c. all-purpose flour
1-1/4 c. water

Blend sugar and shortening together; slowly stir in soup. Sift baking soda, baking powder, cloves, cinnamon, allspice and flour together; add to sugar mixture alternately with water. Mix well; pour into a jelly-roll pan. Bake at 350 degrees for 15 to 20 minutes until top springs back when touched. Cool; top with Lemon Frosting. Makes 12 to 15 servings.

Lemon Frosting:

2 c. powdered sugar
1/2 c. margarine

1 t. lemon extract

Blend together sugar and margarine; add lemon extract. Beat until fluffy.

Don't have a tablecloth big enough for your family reunion? New bedsheets are an economical alternative. Look for patterns to match the theme of your reunion, or choose a plain color that everyone can "autograph" with permanent pens for a special keepsake of the event.

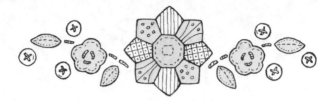

Butterscotch Pie

Marie Hollins
Manitoba, Canada

This pie is a melt-in-your-mouth family favorite!

1-1/4 c. brown sugar, packed
   and divided
3/4 t. salt, divided
4 T. all-purpose flour
3 eggs, separated

2 c. milk, heated just to boiling
   and cooled
1/2 t. vanilla extract
2 T. butter
9-inch pie crust, baked

Sift together 3/4 cup plus 2 tablespoons brown sugar, 1/2 teaspoon salt and flour into the top of a double boiler. Beat egg yolks; add to brown sugar mixture. Gradually add milk; place over hot water in bottom of double boiler. Heat until thick and smooth, stirring constantly. Cover and heat an additional 10 minutes; remove from heat. Add vanilla and butter; mix well. Let cool and pour into pie crust; set aside. Beat egg whites with remaining salt until soft peaks form. Gradually add remaining brown sugar; beat until stiff. Spread over pie, sealing edges. Bake at 325 degrees for 15 to 20 minutes until golden. Makes 6 to 8 servings.

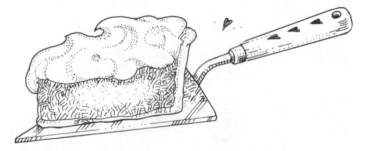

Treat your kids to an old-fashioned delight the next time you bake a pie. Roll out scraps of pie dough, sprinkle with cinnamon sugar and bake for about 10 minutes at 350 degrees. Crunchy and sweet!

Grandma's Bringing
✿ **Dessert** ✿

Oh, Susannah! Pies

Carol Hickman
Kingsport, TN

Who knows why they're called Oh, Susannah! Pies...the name seems to have originated here in Tennessee. I do know that with only 15 minutes of thawing time needed, you'll always have a delicious dessert on hand for unexpected company.

7-oz. pkg. flaked coconut
1 c. chopped pecans
1/2 c. butter
8-oz. pkg. cream cheese, softened
14-oz. can sweetened condensed milk

16-oz. container frozen whipped topping, thawed
3 9-inch graham cracker crusts
12-oz. jar caramel topping

Combine coconut, pecans and butter in a saucepan. Heat until golden; set aside. Mix together cream cheese, condensed milk and whipped topping; divide evenly between pie crusts. Divide coconut mixture; sprinkle evenly over each pie. Drizzle pies with caramel topping; cover pies and freeze. Thaw 15 minutes before serving. Makes 3 pies; each pie serves 6 to 8.

The lid from Grandmother's favorite cookie tin makes a charming wall clock. Pick up a clock kit from your local craft store...it's easy. Simply drill the center hole, insert the movement and hands and add self-adhesive numbers.

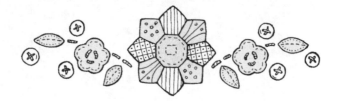

Tina's Famous Ice Cream Cake

Heather Hatter
Winchester, VA

Be creative! Try different flavors of ice cream, sandwich cookies and whipped topping.

1/2 c. butter, melted
20-oz. pkg. chocolate sandwich
   cookies, crushed and divided
1/2 gal. favorite flavor ice cream,
   softened

12-oz. jar hot fudge topping
12-oz. jar caramel topping
16-oz. container frozen whipped
   topping, thawed

Combine butter and cookie crumbs, reserving 1/2 cup crumbs; press into a 13"x9" baking pan. Freeze for one hour. Spread ice cream over frozen crumb mixture. Freeze an additional 15 to 20 minutes. Heat hot fudge topping in microwave for one minute; spread over ice cream and freeze for 5 minutes. Heat caramel topping in microwave for one minute; spread over hot fudge layer. Freeze for 15 to 20 minutes. Spread whipped topping over caramel layer; top with reserved cookie crumbs. Freeze overnight. Makes 12 servings.

Make a celebration plate for special goodies. Check your local craft store for a clear glass plate and for craft paints designed especially for glass. Edge the plate with a special message like "Grandmother's Coconut Cake" or "Happy Birthday." A fun project for kids and adults alike!

Grandma's Bringing Dessert

Pecan Balls with Fudge Sauce

Nicki Baltz
Zionsville, IN

My mother-in-law taught me to make this scrumptious dessert when I was a newlywed.

1/2 gal. vanilla ice cream, softened
2 c. chopped pecans

Optional: frozen whipped topping, thawed and maraschino cherries

Scoop ice cream into 8 to 10 orange-size balls. Roll in pecans; place in a baking pan, cover and freeze. At serving time, top with Fudge Sauce and, if desired, whipped topping and cherries. Makes 8 to 10 servings.

Fudge Sauce:

1/2 c. butter
2 sqs. unsweetened baking chocolate

2/3 c. sugar
1/2 c. evaporated milk
1/2 t. vanilla extract

Melt butter and chocolate in a saucepan over low heat. Add sugar; stir about 2 to 3 minutes until smooth. Immediately add evaporated milk and vanilla; mix well and bring to a slow boil. Remove from heat; let cool before pouring over Pecan Balls.

A well-loved teapot that's been handed down to you makes an endearing vase for cut flowers. Try old-fashioned blooms like daisies, coreopsis, bachelor buttons, zinnia and larkspur.

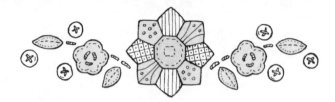

Lil's Blackberry Pie

Lillian Kane
Dansville, NY

Every July, my husband grabs his berry basket and goes blackberry picking with me so he can have blackberry pie all winter long. Last year I made 32 blackberry pies...that's a lot of picking!

3/4 c. sugar, divided
2 T. plus 1 t. cinnamon, divided
2 9-inch pie crusts
4 c. blackberries, divided

1/2 c. water, divided
1/8 t. nutmeg
2 T. cornstarch
Optional: vanilla ice cream

Mix together 1/4 cup sugar and 2 tablespoons cinnamon. Place one crust in a 9" pie pan; sprinkle pie crust with sugar mixture. Pour 2 cups blackberries into crust; sprinkle with 1/4 cup sugar and set aside. Place remaining berries in a heavy saucepan; add 1/2 cup water and remaining sugar. Bring to a boil over medium heat; reduce heat and simmer 10 minutes until berries are juicy. Add remaining cinnamon and nutmeg; stir well. Stir cornstarch into remaining water; add to berries a little at a time, stirring constantly until thick. If necessary, mix and add another batch of cornstarch and water. Pour hot mixture over berries in pie crust. Let cool for 10 to 15 minutes; add second crust, or make a lattice crust if desired. Crimp edges to seal; cut slits in crust to vent. Bake at 375 degrees for about 40 minutes or until golden. Serve with vanilla ice cream, if desired. Makes 6 to 8 servings.

Top pies with pastry cut into quilt-patch shapes for a change from solid crusts. Brush the cut-outs with milk and sprinkle with sugar for a festive touch.

Blueberry-Cream Cheese Pie

Jennifer Eveland-Kupp
Temple, PA

A delicious no-cook pie...make it when you don't want to heat up the kitchen.

2 8-oz. pkgs. cream cheese,
   softened
1/2 c. sugar
1 t. vanilla extract

1/2 t. nutmeg
9-inch graham cracker crust
21-oz. can blueberry pie filling
1 t. lemon juice

Blend together cream cheese, sugar, vanilla and nutmeg. Spread evenly into crust; set aside. Combine pie filling and lemon juice; spoon over cream cheese mixture. Chill until ready to serve. Serves 6 to 8.

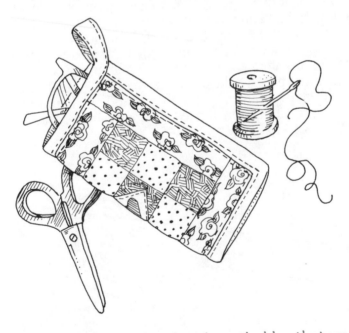

Grandma always had a handmade potholder that was too special to use. Turn it into a handy eyeglass case...simply fold together, with the tab at top, and stitch along 2 edges.

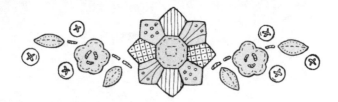

Grandma Pruitt's Angel Food Cake

Debbie Roberts
Columbus, IN

My grandmother made angel food birthday cakes each year for my cousins and me. I stayed with her daily from an early age until I entered school, so I got to help make lots of these cakes.

1 c. cake flour
1-1/2 c. sugar, divided
1-1/4 c. egg whites, at room
　temperature

1/4 t. salt
1-1/4 t. cream of tartar
1 t. vanilla extract
1/4 t. almond extract

Sift together flour and 1/2 cup sugar; set aside. Beat together egg whites, salt and cream of tartar until glossy peaks form. Sprinkle remaining sugar over egg whites, 4 tablespoons at a time, beating 25 strokes by hand after each addition. Beat in vanilla and almond extracts for 10 strokes. Sift 1/4 cup of the flour mixture over egg whites; beat 15 strokes. Fold remaining flour mixture into egg whites; beat 10 strokes after last addition. Pour into an ungreased tube pan lined with wax paper; bake at 375 degrees for 30 to 35 minutes. Remove from oven; invert pan and let stand one hour until cool. Loosen edges with a knife if needed; remove from pan onto cake plate. Serves 15 to 20.

Freshen up a vintage metal cake carrier...still the best way to carry a cake! Lightly sand, then spray with acrylic paint. Decorate with paint pens and colorful stickers.

Granny Pursley's Pound Cake

Sandra Pursley
Ooltewah, TN

Granny always made this cake for church dinners.

2 c. sugar
1 c. oil
2 c. all-purpose flour

5 T. milk
1 T. vanilla extract
5 eggs

Combine all ingredients in a mixing bowl, beating in eggs one at a time. Pour into a greased 10" Bundt® pan. Bake at 350 degrees for 30 minutes; reduce temperature to 325 degrees and bake an additional 30 minutes. Serves 8 to 10.

Make Grandma's glass flower vases sparkle as she did...partially fill with vinegar, let stand several hours, then add a little rice and shake vigorously. Rinse and fill with fresh flowers.

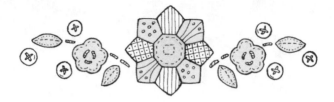

Momma's Rice Pudding

Marcy Abbale
Eugene, OR

This recipe has been in my family forever! My great-grandmother from Norway passed it down to my grandmother, then my mother and now to me. I gave it to my daughter when she was married. It is the creamiest and warms your tummy!

2 c. water
1 c. long-cooking rice, uncooked
1 t. salt
1 T. oil
1-1/2 qts. whole or 2% milk

2 eggs
1/2 c. sugar
Optional: 3/4 c. raisins
Garnish: cinnamon; vanilla ice cream or half-and-half

Combine water, rice, salt and oil in a heavy saucepan. Bring to a boil; reduce heat, cover and simmer for 15 minutes. Turn off heat; leave in pan for 10 minutes. Stir milk into rice mixture. Bring to a boil; reduce heat to low, cooking and stirring every 5 to 10 minutes with a wooden spoon for about one hour. Beat eggs in a small bowl; stir in sugar, then add to rice mixture along with raisins, if using, and cook for 5 minutes longer. Sprinkle with cinnamon and serve warm, topped with vanilla ice cream or half-and-half. Makes 6 to 8 servings.

If Grandma never wrote down her recipes, you can still make a scrapbook of family food memories. Ask for descriptions of favorite dishes...how they smelled, tasted and looked when they were served. Collect them in a scrapbook and add special photos of family meals. Who knows, maybe someone who looks at your scrapbook will have the recipes you miss!

Grandma's Bringing Dessert

Lemon Pudding

Dorothy Baldauf
Crystal Lake, IL

My family has enjoyed this light, not-too-sweet dessert for years.

2 T. butter, softened
1 c. sugar
2 T. all-purpose flour
juice of 1-1/2 lemons

zest of 1 lemon
2 eggs, separated
1 c. milk

Blend together butter and sugar. Add flour, lemon juice and zest. Add egg yolks; beat well and add milk. Stiffly beat egg whites; fold into mixture. Pour into a buttered 2-quart baking dish. Set dish in a baking pan filled with water; bake at 350 degrees for 35 minutes. Makes 6 to 8 servings.

If you've always wanted to quilt but it seems like such a big project...start small! A single 12-inch square of a simple pattern like Nine Patch makes a breadbasket topper with country charm.

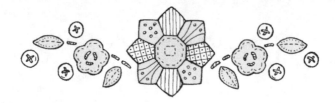

Grandpa House's Taffy

Jolene Behrend
Harlan, IA

My sisters and I lost our grandmother at an early age, but we cherish our memories of pulling taffy with Grandpa during the summers he spent with us.

1 c. water
4 c. sugar
2/3 c. light corn syrup

1 c. whipping cream
1 T. vanilla extract
1 c. chopped walnuts

Bring water to a boil in a saucepan; add sugar and syrup and stir just until dissolved. Lower heat and cook to soft-ball stage, 234 to 243 degrees on a candy thermometer. Slowly add whipping cream and heat mixture to hard-ball stage, 250 to 269 degrees on a candy thermometer. Remove from heat; add vanilla. Pour mixture into 2 buttered jelly-roll pans; let cool. Sprinkle nuts on top; let cool until able to handle. Pull taffy repeatedly until light-colored and hard to pull, then pull into long 1/2-inch thick strips. Cut with scissors into one-inch pieces. Arrange on wax paper; store at room temperature. Makes about 8 dozen.

Fill small shadow boxes with whimsical collections of items like baby bracelets, buttons and small photos...arrange in groupings for a precious wall display.

Grandma's Bringing Dessert

Grandma Jennie's Angel Crisps

Jen Sell
Farmington, MN

Recently I was able to borrow my grandmother's recipe box. It took me 6 weeks to copy down every single recipe, but it was worth it! This was one of my dad's favorite cookies.

1 c. shortening
1/2 c. brown sugar, packed
3/4 c. sugar, divided
1 egg
1 t. vanilla extract

2 c. all-purpose flour
1/2 t. baking soda
1/2 t. cream of tartar
1/2 t. salt
Optional: chopped walnuts

Blend together shortening, brown sugar and 1/2 cup sugar. Mix in egg and vanilla; add flour, baking soda, cream of tartar, salt and nuts, if desired. Form into 1-1/2 inch balls; roll in remaining sugar. Arrange on an ungreased baking sheet; bake at 375 degrees for 10 to 12 minutes or until golden around the edges. Makes 2 dozen.

Drape one of Grandma's vintage hankies over a small lampshade...so pretty and simple too! Place a low-wattage bulb in the lamp to prevent overheating.

Cottage Pudding

Mary Rasefske
Broadalbin, NY

This recipe has been a family tradition since my great-grandmother was a new bride. My sister, brother and I always asked for it when Mom gave us a special treat. Stir in thinly sliced apples, peaches, blueberries or mini chocolate chips for a sweet variation.

1/4 c. shortening
2/3 c. sugar
1 egg
1/2 c. milk

1/2 t. vanilla extract
1-1/2 c. all-purpose flour
2 t. baking powder
1/2 t. salt

Blend together shortening and sugar; add egg, milk and vanilla and blend until smooth. Add remaining ingredients; mix well. Pour into a greased and floured 9"x9" baking pan; bake at 350 degrees for 25 minutes. Serve with warm sauce. Serves 6 to 8.

Sauce:

1 c. sugar
1 T. all-purpose flour
1 T. butter
1/8 t. salt

1 c. water
vanilla extract and nutmeg
to taste

Blend sugar, flour, butter and salt; set aside. Bring water to a boil in a saucepan; stir in sugar mixture. Reduce heat and cook slowly until sauce thickens. Add vanilla and nutmeg to taste.

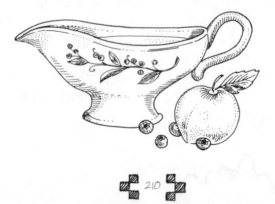

Grandma's Bringing
❀ Dessert ❀

Gramma's Peach Dumplings

Trish Hughes
Albuquerque, NM

This is a very old Czechoslovakian recipe from our family...a mouthwatering treat when peaches are in season!

1 T. butter, softened	1 c. milk
1 T. sugar	10 peaches
2 eggs	1/2 t. salt
3 c. all-purpose flour	Garnish: melted butter, sugar
1 t. baking powder	

Blend butter, sugar and eggs on low speed with a hand mixer; set aside. In a second bowl, mix together flour and baking powder. Alternately add flour mixture and milk to egg mixture, blending after each addition. With floured hands, completely cover each peach with a handful of dough; set aside. Fill a stockpot with water; add salt, cover and bring to a boil. Add peaches a few at a time, cover and boil for 15 minutes; do not overboil or lift cover while boiling. Serve with melted butter and sugar on top. Serves 10.

Make teddy bears for the grandchildren from Grandpa's soft flannel shirts. Whether you use the simplest pattern or a more elaborate one, they will treasure these endearing reminders of Grandpa.

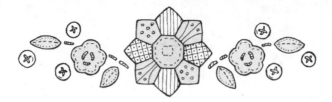

Mother's No-Bake Cookies

Betty Cook
Gilmer, TX

These are delicious...almost like candy!

4 c. sugar
1 c. margarine
1 c. milk
6 T. baking cocoa

1 c. crunchy peanut butter
6 c. instant oats, uncooked
Optional: 1 c. walnuts,
    1 c. flaked coconut

Combine sugar, margarine, milk and cocoa; mix well. Bring to a boil over low heat; boil for one minute. Add peanut butter, stirring until melted. Add oats and, if desired, nuts or coconut. Mix well; drop by teaspoonfuls onto wax paper. Makes 6 to 7 dozen.

Soft Peanut Butter Cookies

Brenda Tranka
Amboy, IL

This recipe is from my sister, who recently passed away. She loved to write down recipes...I framed several of them to remember her by.

1 c. sugar
1 c. creamy peanut butter

1 egg, slightly beaten
1 t. vanilla extract

Combine all ingredients; mix well. Drop by teaspoonfuls onto a baking sheet; use a fork to press a criss-cross pattern on top of each cookie. Bake at 325 degrees for 10 minutes or until golden. Let cool before removing from sheet. Makes 2 to 3 dozen.

Line a pretty basket with one of Grandma's vintage doilies or tea towels to deliver a special gift of cookies.

Grandma's Bringing
🌸 Dessert 🌸

Mom's Chocolate Pie

Debbie Driggers
Greenville, TX

This pie was always a holiday tradition in my family. Knowing that my husband loved chocolate pie, my mother always made an extra pie and hid it for him.

1/2 c. all-purpose flour
1-1/4 c. sugar
3 T. baking cocoa
3 eggs, separated and divided
2 c. water

1/4 c. butter
1/8 t. salt
1 t. vanilla extract
1 t. butter extract
9-inch pie crust, baked

Mix flour, sugar and cocoa; blend in egg yolks and set aside. Heat water in a saucepan with butter and salt until butter is melted; let cool slightly. Add water mixture to flour mixture; heat until thick. Let cool; add extracts. Pour into baked pie crust. Spread meringue over filling, sealing edges carefully. Bake at 350 degrees for 10 minutes or until lightly golden. Serves 6 to 8.

Never-Fail Meringue:

1 T. cornstarch
2 T. cold water
1/2 c. boiling water
3 egg whites

6 T. sugar
1/8 t. salt
1 t. vanilla extract

Blend cornstarch and cold water in a saucepan. Add boiling water; continue heating until clear and thickened. Let stand until completely cooled. Beat egg whites with electric mixer on high speed until foamy; gradually add sugar and beat until stiff but not dry. Reduce mixer to low speed; add salt and vanilla. Gradually beat in cold cornstarch mixture. Increase mixer speed to high and beat well.

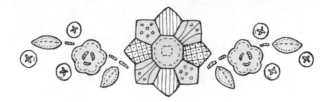

Poor Man's Cake

Linda Behling
Cecil, PA

This recipe was passed down from my husband's great-grandmother.
It's from the Depression so it calls for cupboard staples and no eggs.
It smells sooo good when it's baking!

12-oz. pkg. raisins
3 c. water, divided
1/2 c. chopped walnuts
1/2 c. candied cherries, chopped
1/2 c. shortening
2 c. sugar

4 c. all-purpose flour
1 t. nutmeg
1 t. cinnamon
1 t. ground cloves
1 T. baking soda

Simmer raisins in 2 cups water until raisins become plump; do not
drain. Add nuts, cherries, and shortening to raisin mixture; mix well.
Stir in sugar and remaining water and let cool. Add flour, nutmeg,
cinnamon, cloves and baking soda. Mix well; pour into 2 greased
9"x5" loaf pans. Bake at 350 degrees for one hour. Makes 10 to
12 servings.

Turn faceted glass candy dishes into sparkly candles...just fill
with scented candle gel or wax chips and add a wick.
Group together on a mirrored tray for extra sparkle.

Grandma's Bringing
❀ Dessert ❀

Charlotte's Chocolate Sheet Cake

Terri Lock
Waverly, MO

*My mother-in-law is famous for this cake in our family...all
22 grandchildren request it when we get together!*

1 c. margarine
1 c. water
4 T. baking cocoa
2 c. all-purpose flour
2 c. sugar

1 t. baking soda
1/8 t. salt
1/2 c. buttermilk
2 eggs, beaten

Place margarine, water and cocoa in a saucepan. Heat until margarine
melts; let cool. In a mixing bowl, combine flour, sugar, baking soda
and salt; mix well. Add margarine mixture, buttermilk and eggs to
flour mixture; stir well. Spread in a greased jelly-roll pan; bake for
20 minutes at 400 degrees. Serves 15 to 20.

Full-page food advertisements from vintage ladies' magazines
look appealing framed in your kitchen. Perhaps you'll find one
featuring Grandma's all-time favorite recipe!

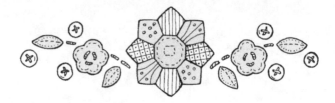

Pineapple Upside-Down Cake

Retha Falkenberry
Broken Arrow, OK

My late mother's recipe for Pineapple Upside-Down Cake is one of the best I've ever tasted. She found it in a cookbook my father bought for her from a door-to-door salesman, way back in the 1930's.

1-1/3 c. cake flour
1-1/2 t. baking powder
1/4 t. salt
3 eggs, separated and divided
1 c. sugar, divided

1 t. vanilla extract
20-oz. can pineapple slices,
   1/3 c. juice reserved
1/4 c. butter
1 c. brown sugar, packed

Sift together flour, baking powder and salt; set aside. Beat egg whites until stiff but not dry; gradually beat in 1/2 cup sugar, 2 tablespoons at a time. Set aside. Beat egg yolks until thick and lemon colored; add remaining sugar and vanilla. Continue beating until very thick; slowly add reserved pineapple juice, stirring constantly. Gently fold in egg white mixture and then dry ingredients, sifting about 1/4 cup at a time over the surface. Set aside. Melt butter and brown sugar in a cast iron skillet. Arrange a single layer of pineapple slices in bottom of skillet; pour in batter. Bake at 350 degrees for 40 to 45 minutes or until cake springs back when pressed. Invert onto cake plate. Serves 6 to 8.

Bring Grandma's Sunday going-to-church hats out of their
boxes and arrange several on hat stands
for a whimsical display.

Grandma's Bringing
Dessert

Red Pop Cake

Dianne Gregory
Sheridan, AR

We love this cake with its secret ingredient...red pop!

2 c. all-purpose flour
1-1/2 c. sugar
3-1/2 t. baking powder
1 t. salt
1/4 c. butter, softened
1/4 c. shortening
2 c. milk, divided
1-1/2 t. vanilla extract

3 eggs
3-oz. pkg. strawberry gelatin
  mix
12-oz. can red pop
3-oz. pkg. instant vanilla
  pudding mix
8-oz. container frozen whipped
  topping, thawed

Combine flour, sugar, baking powder, salt, butter, shortening, one cup milk, vanilla and eggs; beat on low speed until well mixed. Beat on high speed an additional 3 minutes. Spread in a greased and floured 13"x9" cake pan. Bake at 350 degrees for 40 to 45 minutes. Remove from oven; poke holes in cake with the handle of a wooden spoon. Stir together gelatin mix and pop; pour over cake and refrigerate. Prepare pudding according to package instructions, using the remaining milk. Combine with whipped topping; spoon over cooled cake. Cover and refrigerate cake until serving. Makes 8 to 10 servings.

Dress up a plain cake topping...sprinkle on homemade colored sugar! Just put 1/2 cup sugar in a jar with a tight lid, add 2 drops food coloring, close the lid and shake well for about a minute. Spread on wax paper to dry.

Potluck
You're Invited

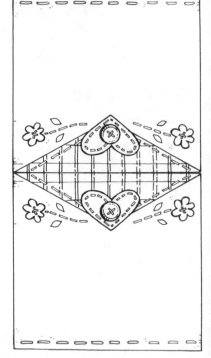

Cut-outs for your reunion or potluck...just copy, color and cut!

Recipe:
Servings:

A picture frame to enlarge, copy & color!

Index

Index

Index

Mom's Apple Pie ♡ Grandma's Chicken & Noodles

Vickie's Deviled Eggs

Doris's Potato Salad ⦿ JoAnn's Baked Beans

Fried Catfish ◈ can't eat another bite!